take 6
ingredients

CONRAD GALLAGHER

take 6 ingredients

100 ingenious recipes to create
simple, delicious meals

with photographs by Gus Filgate

KYLE BOOKS

To Minoo

I dedicate this book to you for making my world a better place and for being there when all others had gone.

This edition published in 2004 by Kyle Books,
an imprint of Kyle Cathie Limited.
general.enquiries@kyle-cathie.com
www.kylecathie.com

Distributed by National Book Network
4501 Forbes Blvd., Suite 200
Lanham, MD 20706
Phone: (301) 459 3366
Fax: (301) 429 5746

ISBN 1-904920-00-4

Text © 2003 Conrad Gallagher
Photography © 2003 Gus Filgate
Book design © 2003 Kyle Cathie Limited

Senior Editor Muna Reyal
Designer Geoff Hayes
Photographer Gus Filgate
Home economists Annie Nicolls, David Morgan and Jenny White
Styling Penny Markham
Production Sha Huxtable

The Library of Congress Cataloguing-in-Publication Data is available on file.

Colour reproduction by Sang Choy
Printed and bound in Singapore by Star Standard

contents

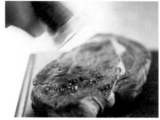

introduction

To cook is to have fun. I'm a chef so I would say that, but cooking for family and friends is a real treat so long as you don't have to assemble a huge list of ingredients before you get to put a pot on the stove. That's why I've written this book – to show what can be done with just a few ingredients and which make really delicious meals.

Oh well, you'll cheat and have a load of store cupboard ingredients too, I hear you cry… oh, how I wish! Time and again I was brought back to my original concept by firm editors. Some people have written books on the concept of 3 ingredients, but I maintain that it's difficult to create interesting dishes with such constraint. I fought for eight or ten and, in the end, settled for that magical A. A. Milne figure of 6. There's sufficient scope yet little to make you feel a slave to the kitchen.

In my store cupboard are three ingredients which I hope are contained in your store cupboard too: they are salt (preferably Maldon sea salt); black pepper (preferably freshly ground peppercorns which you've bought in the last two weeks) and olive oil (preferably the best quality you can afford). Beyond that, no recipe in this book will command more than 6 ingredients.

If you don't have to spend time digging out ingredients (or hopping off to the shops to buy endless lists of them), you will have more time to enjoy assembling those few that you do have. And I hope that you will buy the best quality that you can find. One of my favourite shellfish is the scallop and nowhere is freshness and quality so obviously seen; a tired beast from the supermarket shelf is a Michelin-star away from those I go diving for – hand-picked scallops fresh off the Irish coast of Co. Cork and Donegal – light years away from the dredged ones in terms of flavor. Organic is important. Being a chef I shoot for the best, and that brings me to pace and variety in a meal. I hope that, in these 100+ recipes, you will find dishes with simple flavors – Roasted Poussin with just a flavor of chorizo and a side dish of parsnip puree is sheer delight – to more complex dishes such as Tagliatelle with Roasted Chicken Leg, Mushrooms and Chile, where the shiitake combined with the chile and fresh coriander give the dish a real depth and zing which makes you go back for more and more and more. Cooking as I am now in New York gives me chances to experiment even more – bold flavors, a rich palette of wonderful fresh vegetables and fruits, and an excitement that springs off every sidewalk I go down and every bar and local restaurant I frequent.

The chapters are organised by course of the meal. Straightforward and simple, I hope. Enjoy making these recipes as much as I've enjoyed devising them.

Conrad Gallagher

appetizers

This recipe has to be the height of decadence and tastes sublime. It literally takes minutes to make and not that much longer to devour. Make it for someone you love.

scrambled eggs
with foie gras, truffle and chives

SERVES 4

4 slices (3 oz.) foie gras ●
(goose or duck liver)

4 eggs ●

$^{1}/_{3}$ cup ($^{3}/_{4}$ stick) ●
unsalted butter

$^{1}/_{3}$ cup ($3^{1}/_{2}$ fl.oz.) heavy cream ●

4 tablespoons snipped ●
fresh chives

1 black truffle, thinly sliced ●

Heat a heavy-based pan until very hot. Season the foie gras. Add to the pan and sear for 30 seconds to 1 minute on each side until just tender and caramelized.

Meanwhile, break the eggs into a bowl, season and lightly beat with a fork. Heat the butter and cream in a pan. Add the eggs and cook over a medium heat, stirring all the time, for a minute or two until the eggs are half set.

Remove the pan from the heat and add the chives and truffle shavings. Keep stirring, returning the pan to the heat if necessary, until the eggs are soft and creamy.

Spoon the scrambled eggs on to warmed serving plates and arrange a slice of foie gras to the side of each one. Serve immediately.

You can use ceps instead of wild mushrooms, but if ceps have been collected soon after rain they may exude a lot of moisture whilst cooking. If so, sauté until there is no more than a tablespoon of liquid remaining, then continue with the recipe.

pan-fried wild mushrooms
with parmesan and thyme butter

SERVES 4

3 cups (8 oz.) wild mushrooms, ●
wiped clean and stalks trimmed

2 tablespoons olive oil

Knob of unsalted butter ●

1 tablespoon fresh thyme leaves ●

1 cup (9 fl.oz.) heavy cream ●

2 tablespoons snipped ●
fresh chives

¹/₃ cup (1 oz.) Parmesan shavings ●

Cut the mushrooms into thin slices. Heat the oil in a skillet; when hot, add the mushrooms and sauté for 2–3 minutes or until golden brown and completely tender.

Add the butter and thyme to the pan and season to taste. Once the butter starts to melt, stir in the cream and chives. Cook for another 2–3 minutes until slightly reduced, stirring occasionally.

Divide the mushroom mixture among warmed wide-rimmed bowls and scatter the Parmesan shavings on top. Serve immediately with some crusty bread, if liked.

take 6
ingredients | appetizers

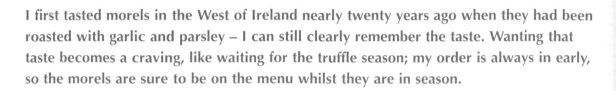

I first tasted morels in the West of Ireland nearly twenty years ago when they had been roasted with garlic and parsley – I can still clearly remember the taste. Wanting that taste becomes a craving, like waiting for the truffle season; my order is always in early, so the morels are sure to be on the menu whilst they are in season.

asparagus
with fresh morels and puff pastry

SERVES 4

9 oz. puff pastry, thawed if frozen ●

2¼ lbs. white asparagus spears (about 24) ●

1 egg yolk, lightly beaten ●

2 tablespoons olive oil

1 shallot, chopped ●

3 cups (9 oz.) fresh morel mushrooms, well washed and stalks trimmed ●

1 cup (9 fl.oz.) heavy cream ●

On a clean, lightly floured surface, roll out the puff pastry to ½-inch thickness and then cut out four rectangles, each about 4 x 6 inches. Transfer to a baking sheet and leave to rest for one hour in the fridge.

Preheat the oven to 400°F. Peel the asparagus spears and trim down into 4-inch lengths. Cook in a pan of boiling salted water for 8–10 minutes or until al dente. If you tie the asparagus in small bundles you will avoid damaging their tips whilst they are cooking. Drain, refresh quickly under cold running water and set aside.

Meanwhile, brush the pastry with the beaten egg yolk and bake for 10 minutes until crisp and golden brown. Heat the olive oil in a pan and sweat the shallot for a minute or two to soften, stirring. Add the morels and continue to sweat for another minute or so, then cover and simmer gently for 10 minutes or until the morels are completely tender. Using a slotted spoon, transfer to the morels to a warmed bowl and keep warm, reserving the remaining shallot and morel cooking juices in the pan.

Pour the cream into the pan with the shallots and morel cooking juices and cook over a high heat until the juice has been reduced by half, stirring occasionally. Return the morels to the sauce and season to taste.

Using a sharp knife, carefully split each puff pastry rectangle in half to create two thin rectangles. Arrange the four bottom rectangles on serving plates. Place six asparagus tips on each rectangle and spoon over the morel mixture, then cover each one with the remaining rectangle of pastry, presentation side up. Flash quickly in the oven to ensure the dish is completely heated through and serve at once.

take 6
ingredients | appetizers

Very stylish, very easy to make and very delicious: the perfect starter! There is now a wide variety of mixed salad bags in every major supermarket and I'm sure we all have our own favorites. However, a garden salad with watercress, with its peppery bite, works particularly well with the other ingredients. It is important to buy a properly smoked chicken from a good delicatessen or supplier.

smoked chicken and avocado

SERVES 6

1 whole smoked chicken ●

About ¾ cup (7 fl.oz.) lemon ●
mayonnaise (preferably
home-made)

3 firm, ripe avocados ●

½ cup (4 fl.oz.) hazelnut oil ●

1 tablespoon white ●
wine vinegar

1½ cups (4 oz.) mixed ●
herb salad

Strip the chicken meat from the carcass and cut into small dice. Place in a bowl and add enough of the mayonnaise to bind. Season to taste.

Halve, remove pit and peel each avocado. Cut the flesh into slices and fan out in a circle on serving plates.

Take a 2½-inch ring mold and gently place on top of each portion of avocado. Fill with the smoked chicken mixture and carefully remove the mold. Place the hazelnut oil and white wine vinegar in a screw-topped bottle, season and shake until well combined.

Place the salad leaves in a bowl, season and add enough of the dressing to coat, tossing lightly to combine. Arrange a small pile of dressed leaves on top of each salad and drizzle around a little more of the dressing to serve.

take 6
ingredients | appetizers

pastrami-style salmon
with herb oil

1 large 12 oz. salmon fillet ●
(not from the tail end)

1 tablespoon coriander seeds ●

2 lemons ●

3/4 cup (7 fl.oz.) olive oil

4 tablespoons chopped mixed ●
herbs (such as dill, cilantro
and chervil)

3 level tablespoons (2 1/2 oz.)
coarse sea salt

3 tablespoons Dijon mustard ●

3 1/2 tablespoons (2 fl.oz.) ●
sour cream

Place half the lemon juice in a screw-topped bottle with the olive oil and three tablespoons of the herbs. Season generously and shake well to combine, then store in the fridge for 2–3 days to allow the flavors to develop.

Preheat the broiler. Skin the salmon, then run your fingers against the grain of the flesh and remove the pin bones with tweezers. Place the coriander seeds on a baking tray and toast under the broiler for a few minutes. Allow to cool, then crush in a pestle and mortar until coarsely ground. Grate the rind from one of the lemons and set aside, then squeeze out the juice from both.

Place the crushed coriander seeds in a bowl and add the salt, reserved lemon rind and a good grinding of black pepper. Lay out a double layer of plastic wrap at least twice the size of the salmon and scatter over half the salt mixture and then sprinkle half of the remaining lemon juice on top. Cover with the salmon and scatter over the remaining salt mixture, finishing with the rest of the lemon juice. Wrap well with the plastic wrap, place on a tray and chill for 24 hours.

Unwrap the salmon, then scrape off and discard the first marinade. Stir the remaining one tablespoon of herbs into the mustard. Lay out a fresh piece of plastic wrap as before and smear the top of the salmon with half of the mustard mixture. Place the smeared side of the salmon down on the plastic wrap and smear the other side using the rest of the mustard mixture. Wrap tightly in the plastic wrap, place on a tray and chill for another 24 hours.

Remove the salmon from the fridge and slice as thinly as possible. Arrange a few slices in the center of each serving plate. Remove the herb oil from the fridge and shake well to combine, then drizzle a little on to each plate. Dot the sour cream around the edges of the plates to serve.

take 6
ingredients | appetizers

Scallops are sweet and succulent and lend themselves to the simplest of dishes. So what could be more perfect than a salad of arugula with seared scallops wrapped in Parma ham, finished with a fresh, vibrant arugula dressing. Here the scallops are sautéed in a hot skillet in which a very small amount of butter has been melted, giving the Parma ham a really crisp and salty exterior.

scallops

wrapped in parma ham with arugula salad and arugula sauce

SERVES 4

10 large fresh scallops ●

10 slices Parma ham ●

5 cups (14 oz.) arugula ●

1/2 cup (4 fl.oz.) olive oil ●

Juice of 1/2 lemon ●

Knob of unsalted butter ●

Detach the corals from the scallops and discard or use them in a sauce. Cut each scallop horizontally into two even-sized discs and set aside. Cut the Parma ham into 1/2-inch strips just long enough to go around the scallop, then cut any trimmings into small dice and reserve. Wrap two strips of Parma ham around each scallop in a criss-cross fashion.

To make the arugula sauce, place 31/2 oz. of arugula in a food processor or blender with the olive oil and lemon juice. Season and whizz until smooth, then transfer to a jug and season to taste.

Heat a heavy skillet. Add the butter and then add the wrapped scallops, presentation side down and cook for about 30 seconds on each side. Divide the remaining arugula among the serving plates and arrange the scallops on top. Drizzle over the arugula sauce and scatter over the reserved Parma ham dice to serve.

take 6
ingredients | appetizers

Ask your fishmonger to open the oysters for you, you'll just need to double check that there are no bits of broken shell inside before using them. Alternatively you could always try having a go yourself, they really are quite simple once you get the hang of them. An oyster knife is a very good investment if they are something that you are intending on cooking regularly.

oysters
with caviar, radish and cucumber

SERVES 4

20 oysters (native, if possible) ●

½ cucumber ●

10 radishes ●

Juice of 2 lemons ●

¼ teaspoon sugar ●

1 tablespoon (¾ oz.) caviar ●
(Sevruga, if possible)

Scrub the oyster shells then place one, wrapped in a clean dish towel on a firm surface with the flattest shell uppermost and the hinge pointing towards you. Gripping the oyster firmly, insert an oyster knife into the gap in the hinge and twist to snap the shells apart.

Slide the blade of the knife along the inside of the upper shell to sever the muscle that keeps the shells together. Lift the lid off the top shell, being careful not to spill any of the juices. Carefully clean away any bits of broken shell and finally run the knife under the oyster to loosen it from the shell. Repeat until all the oysters are opened and then arrange on a tray and place in the fridge until you are ready to serve.

Peel the cucumber and then pare each side into long thin ribbons until you reach the middle seeds, then discard. Layer up the ribbons and using a sharp knife cut into julienne (matchstick) strips, then cut into tiny dice. Place in a bowl, cover with plastic wrap and chill until needed.

Trim the radishes and then pare into strips. Cut into julienne strips just like the cucumber, then cut into tiny dice. Place in a separate bowl, cover with plastic wrap and chill until needed.

To make the lemon dressing, place the lemon juice in a small bowl, add the sugar and stir until dissolved. Arrange five oysters in each of the wide-rimmed bowls and sprinkle the cucumber dice on top, followed by the radish dice. Garnish with tiny spoonfuls of the caviar and drizzle a little of the lemon dressing over each oyster to serve.

Polenta (cornmeal) is extremely versatile and can be flavored with just about anything. It is eaten largely in northern Italy, where it sometimes replaces bread at mealtimes. However, it needs to be well flavored as it can be very bland if made with water and underseasoned. Don't worry if it catches slightly at the bottom of the saucepan, just don't try and incorporate it with the rest of the polenta.

warm herb polenta

with sautéed wild mushrooms and parmesan

SERVES 2

5 cups (2 pints) chicken or vegetable stock

1/4 cup (1/2 stick) unsalted butter

11/3 cups (7 oz.) fine polenta

3 cups (9 oz.) Parmesan shavings, plus extra to garnish

4 tablespoons chopped fresh mixed flat-leaf parsley and basil

11/4 cups (31/2 oz.) mixed wild mushrooms

● Heat the stock and half the butter in a deep-sided, heavy saucepan. Bring to a boil and then reduce the heat until simmering, season to taste. Slowly pour in the polenta in a thin, steady stream, stirring vigorously with a wooden spoon.

● Once all the polenta has been added simmer gently on the lowest possible heat until the mixture is thick and comes away from the sides of the pan, stirring constantly. This should take anywhere between 5 and 45 minutes, depending on the type of polenta you are using. Beat in the Parmesan with three tablespoons of the mixed herbs, then season to taste and keep warm.

● Heat the remaining butter in a skillet, then tip in the mushrooms and season to taste. Sauté for a couple of minutes until tender. Divide the polenta between two warmed wide-rimmed bowls and spoon the mushrooms on top. Garnish with the remaining tablespoon of herbs and Parmesan shavings. Serve at once.

take 6
ingredients | appetizers

An extravagant little dish, but well worth the expense and trouble, I reckon. However it is definitely for the more adventurous. More complicated than most, but get it right and it's a match made in heaven! A crisp brown layer of potatoes containing a moist, buttery interior served with succulent sweetbreads that have been sautéed in butter – needless to say this is also not one for the faint hearted…

carpaccio of potato

with veal sweetbreads

SERVES 4

18 oz. veal sweetbreads ●

1¼ lbs. (about 4 medium) ●
potatoes

½ cup (1 stick) unsalted butter, ●
plus a little extra if necessary

⅓ cup (3½ fl.oz.) hazelnut oil ●

5 teaspoons raspberry vinegar ●

Mixed baby salad leaves ●

Soak the whole sweetbreads in a large bowl of water overnight, changing the water as often as possible. The next morning, blanch the sweetbreads in a saucepan of boiling water for about 5 minutes, then lift out with a slotted spoon and plunge them into a bowl of ice-cold water. Remove the membrane encasing them as well as any fat or other waste and pick over until they are around the size of walnuts. Drain well on paper towels and set aside.

Peel and thinly slice the potatoes with a sharp knife. Heat a large heavy skillet and add 1½ oz. of the butter. Add a layer of the potato slices and cook over a very low heat until tender. Drain the cooked potatoes on paper towels and season with salt, then repeat the process until all the potatoes have been cooked and drained, adding a little more butter if necessary. Wipe out the skillet. Arrange the cooked potato slices in a slightly overlapping layer to make large circles on heatproof serving plates.

Preheat the broiler. To make the vinaigrette, place the hazelnut oil in a small bowl with the raspberry vinegar and seasoning, then whisk to combine and set aside. Reheat the skillet and add the remaining butter, then sear the sweetbreads over a fairly high heat until they are golden brown and completely tender. Season to taste.

Meanwhile, flash the plates with the potato carpaccio under the broiler until the potatoes are golden brown and arrange the sweetbreads around the edge of each plate. Garnish each plate with a small mound of salad leaves and drizzle over a little of the vinaigrette to serve.

take 6
ingredients | appetizers

steamed mussels
with watercress sauce

SERVES 4

2 1/4 lbs. fresh mussels ●

2/3 cup (1/4 pint) white wine ●

1/3 cup (3 1/2 fl.oz.) heavy cream ●

1 bunch of watercress, ●
leaves picked over and
stalks discarded

1/3 cup (1/2 stick) ●
unsalted butter

1/2 lemon ●

Scrub the mussels well, scrape off any barnacles and pull out the beards protruding from between the two closed shells. Discard any that won't close when they are lightly tapped on the work surface.

Place the wine in a large saucepan with a few white peppercorns if you have them and bring to a boil. Add the mussels, then cover and cook, shaking the saucepan every now and then, for about 5 minutes or until all the mussels have opened. Discard any that stay closed.

Tip the mussels into a colander set over a large bowl and then pass the cooking liquid once more through a fine sieve and return to the pan. Keep the mussels warm. Bring the cooking liquid back to a boil, then pour in the cream and tip in the watercress leaves. Cook for 3–4 minutes, stirring occasionally, then ladle the mixture into a food processor or liquidizer. Whizz to a puree, then pass through a sieve into a clean saucepan, thinning the sauce with a little water if it has become too thick.

Place the saucepan on the heat and bring to a gentle simmer, then whisk in the butter and add a squeeze of lemon juice and enough seasoning to taste. Divide the mussels between large wide-rimmed bowls and pour over the sauce. Season with a little black pepper and serve.

Beets have a natural affinity with orange and this recipe capitalizes on it. The "lattes" should be quite a rich pink with a creamy consistency that is speckled with pistachio nuts, suitable for the most elegant of dinners. For the maximum effect, I like to serve them in glass coffee cups. Obviously having a cappuccino maker in the restaurant helps, but don't worry if you don't have access to one. There are a number of decent gadgets available in cookstores which will do a perfectly adequate job.

roasted beet and orange "latte"

SERVES 4

2 cups (1 lb.) fresh small beets, trimmed and peeled

1 tablespoon shelled pistachio nuts

Grated rind and juice of 4 oranges

5 tablespoons (3 fl.oz.) milk

1 small wedge honeydew melon, pitted

● Preheat the oven to 375°F. Wrap the beets in a loose pouch of aluminum foil, sealing the top tightly. Place on a roasting pan and roast for 30–40 minutes until completely tender.

● Heat a small frying skillet. Add the pistachio nuts and cook for a couple of minutes until toasted and lightly brown, shaking the pan occasionally to prevent them from burning.

● Remove the beets from the oven and tip the contents of the aluminum foil pouch into a food processor or liquidizer. Blend to a puree, then with the machine still running, slowly pour in the orange juice and add half of the rind. Finally, pour in two-thirds of the milk until just combined.

● Switch off the machine and season to taste. Pour into heatproof glasses and sprinkle the toasted pistachios on top. Steam the remaining milk using a cappuccino steamer or whisk, and then carefully spoon on top of the beet mixture. Sprinkle over the remaining orange rind, and pare shavings of the melon to top to serve.

take 6
ingredients | appetizers

soups

The honey combines well with the flavor of the parsnips to make this warming soup, best enjoyed in winter – which just happens to be when parsnips are at their best. By the way, if parsnips are large and "woody", cut out the hard center and discard. I like to serve this soup garnished with pickled mackerel fillet, but that, of course, is an optional extra.

parsnip and honey soup

SERVES 4

2 tablespoons olive oil

2 shallots, chopped ●

2 parsnips, diced ●

1 potato, diced ●

2³/₄ cups (1¹/₄ pints) ●
chicken broth

¹/₃ cup (3¹/₂ fl.oz.) heavy cream, ●
plus a little extra to garnish

2 tablespoons clear honey ●

Heat the oil in a large pan and sweat the shallots, parsnips and potato for about 10 minutes until softened, but not colored, stirring occasionally.

Pour the broth into the saucepan with the cream and bring to a boil, then reduce the heat and simmer for another 15–20 minutes or until the parsnips are completely tender, stirring occasionally. Stir in the honey and season to taste.

Puree the soup in a food processor or with a hand-held blender and then pass through a fine sieve into a clean saucepan for a really smooth finish. Reheat gently and season to taste. Ladle into bowls and add a swirl of cream to serve.

Ever since myself and my brothers were paid with a couple of pounds of mussels for a small repair job that we did on a fisherman's boat I have loved this variety of seafood. This is the exact recipe that I prepared that day and I can tell you that there's nothing better than a steaming bowl of mussel soup after a day by the docks.

mussel soup
with fine beans, tomato and coriander

SERVES 4

3 lbs. 5 oz. mussels ●

1¼ cups (½ pint) ● dry white wine

3 tablespoons olive oil

1 onion, finely chopped ●

1½ cups (7 oz.) fine green ● beans, finely chopped

3 plum tomatoes, peeled, ● seeded and diced

1 bunch of fresh cilantro, ● leaves stripped and chopped

Scrub the mussels well, scrape off any barnacles and pull out the beards protruding from between the two closed shells. Discard any that won't close when they are lightly tapped on the work surface.

Heat a large saucepan over a high heat. Tip in the mussels and cover for 10–15 seconds, then pour over the wine and 1¼ cups (½ pint) of water. Add a few white peppercorns if you've got them, then cover and cook, shaking the saucepan every now and then, for 5 minutes or until all the mussels have opened. Discard any that stay closed.

Tip the mussels into a colander set over a large bowl and then pass the cooking liquid once more through a fine sieve and reserve. When the mussels are cool enough to handle, remove the mussel meats from their shells and reserve, discarding the shells.

Heat a saucepan. Add one tablespoon of the olive oil and then add the onion. Cook for a few minutes until softened, then pour in the reserved cooking liquid and bring to a boil. Season to taste. Add the beans, mussels and tomatoes and just warm through. Ladle into warmed wide-rimmed bowls, scatter over the cilantro and drizzle over the remaining olive oil. Serve immediately.

take 6
ingredients | soups

This is a version of the traditional Italian stew of bell peppers and tomatoes that I've made into a soup. It's a great winter warmer that packs a subtle smoky chorizo punch. If you want to make it more substantial simply add 1 cup (7 oz.) of cooked white beans, such as cannelloni or lima and just allow them to warm through at the end of the cooking time. It is also great served with chunks of toasted country-style bread.

chorizo and sweet bell pepper soup

SERVES 4

²/₃ cup (6 oz.) Spanish chorizo, diced

4 sweet bell peppers, pitted and diced (red, yellow or green)

2 large garlic cloves, finely chopped

2 plum tomatoes, peeled, seeded and cut into dice

3³/₄ cups (1¹/₂ pints) chicken broth

2 heaped tablespoons chopped fresh cilantro

Heat a large saucepan. Add the chorizo and sauté for a few minutes or until the chorizo is sizzling and has begun to release its oil. Remove the chorizo with a slotted spoon and drain on paper towels, reserving the oil that is left in the bottom of the saucepan. Set the chorizo aside.

Add the bell peppers to the pan and cook over a fairly high heat for about 10 minutes until just tender and beginning to color around the edges, stirring occasionally. Stir in the garlic and tomatoes and cook for another couple of minutes, stirring occasionally. Pour in the broth, season to taste and bring to a boil. Reduce the heat and simmer for 6–8 minutes or until the bell peppers are completely tender.

Puree the soup in batches in a food processor or with a hand-held blender. Return the soup to a clean saucepan, season to taste and stir in the cilantro. Reheat gently, then ladle into warmed wide-rimmed bowls and scatter over the reserved chorizo. Serve at once.

take 6
ingredients | soups

The natural sweetness of the different kinds of onions give this soup a wonderful flavor. I find the simplest way of peeling the pearl onions is to pour a kettle of boiling water over them and set them aside for a minute or two, then drain and peel once they are cool enough to handle. This soup can be served either warm or ice cold, depending on the season. I also like to make it with young tender spinach leaves, again, depending on the time of year.

watercress soup with sweet onions

SERVES 4

1 tablespoon olive oil

2 tablespoons (1 oz.) leeks, ●
finely chopped

1 shallot, finely chopped ●

2 bunches (1 lb.) watercress, ●
well picked over

1 lb. pearl onions, peeled ●
(about 12)

3¾ cups (1½ pints) chicken or ●
vegetable broth

5 tablespoons (3 fl.oz.) Greek ●
strained yogurt

Heat the oil in a pan. Add the leek and shallot and cook for about 5 minutes or until softened but not browned. Chop the watercress, separating the leaves and stalks. Add the stalks to the saucepan with the pearl onions, cover and cook gently for 10 minutes until the onions are just tender but not colored, shaking the saucepan occasionally.

Pour the broth into the saucepan, season to taste and bring to a boil. Reduce the heat and simmer gently for 8–10 minutes or until the pearl onions are completely tender and the soup has slightly reduced. Add the reserved watercress leaves, keeping some back for garnish, and simmer for 1 minute until just wilted, then remove from the heat.

Puree the soup in batches in a food processor or with a hand-held blender. Pour back into a clean saucepan and whisk in the yogurt, then season to taste and reheat gently to just warm through, if liked. Alternatively, chill for at least two hours. Ladle into wide-rimmed bowls and garnish with the reserved watercress leaves. Serve at once.

This is one of my favorite "empty fridge" recipes that requires little preparation (except for the soaking of the garbanzo beans) and is quickly cooked. Garbanzo beans are difficult to put an exact cooking time on as the older they are, the longer they take. However, I always tend to err on the side of caution as there are few things worse than undercooked garbanzo beans. Of course you could always opt for the canned variety which don't taste as good, but are much less bother.

garbanzo bean, bacon and chile soup

SERVES 6–8

3 cups (1¼ lbs.) dried garbanzo beans

7 oz. piece of bacon

3 tablespoons olive oil

1 large onion, finely chopped

2 garlic cloves, finely chopped

2 long red chiles, pitted and finely chopped

10 cups (4¼ pints) chicken broth (preferably home-made)

Place the garbanzo beans in a large bowl and cover with water. Set aside for 24 hours to soak. Drain the beans and place them in a large saucepan with enough water to cover. Bring to a boil and boil vigorously for 10 minutes, then drain and rinse under cold water – this will eliminate any toxins that they may have. Remove the rind from the bacon and cut the piece in half, then cut half into strips and leave the rest in one whole piece; set aside.

Return the saucepan to the heat and add two tablespoons of the olive oil, then tip in the onion, garlic and chile and sweat for about 5 minutes until slightly colored, stirring occasionally. Add the drained beans and cook for another 2 minutes, stirring. Pour in the broth and add the whole piece of bacon, then bring to a boil. Reduce the heat and simmer gently until the beans are tender – this can take anything from 1½–3 hours, depending on how old the beans are.

Remove the piece of bacon from the garbanzo bean mixture and discard, then puree the soup with a hand-held blender until completely smooth. Season to taste and keep warm. Heat a skillet and add the remaining olive oil. Tip in the reserved bacon strips and cook over a fairly high heat for 2–3 minutes or until golden brown. Drain on paper towels. Ladle the soup into warmed wide-rimmed bowls and scatter the bacon on top. Serve immediately.

take 6
ingredients | soups

Lemon grass is popular in Thai cooking as it imparts a pungent, delicate lemon flavor. As you can see, I like to use it with discretion so that the flavor of this soup is deliciously fragrant. However, it is important to use a good-quality, well-flavored chicken broth to begin with.

lemon grass chile soup

SERVES 4–6

2 tablespoons olive oil

4 shallots, finely chopped ●

2 lemon grass stalks, trimmed ●
and finely chopped

2 garlic cloves, finely chopped ●

4 cups (1¾ pints) chicken broth ●

¾ cup (7 fl.oz.) heavy cream ●

½ red chile, pitted and ●
finely chopped

Heat the oil in a large saucepan. Add the shallots, lemon grass and garlic and sweat for about 5 minutes until the mixture has softened but not colored, stirring occasionally.

Pour the broth into the saucepan and bring to a boil, then reduce the heat and simmer for 6–8 minutes to allow the flavors to combine. Season to taste.

Puree the soup in a food processor or with a hand-held blender and then return to a clean saucepan. Pour in the cream and stir in the chile and reheat gently to warm through. Season to taste and ladle into warmed wide-rimmed bowls. Serve at once.

take 6
ingredients | soups

This is a delicate, intensely flavored clear soup. For a crystal-clear finish, clarify the soup at the end of cooking. The golden rules for this are: first remove all fat from the broth; then stir in one egg white and one rinsed and crushed egg shell and keep stirring until the soup begins to simmer and the egg white begins to form a crust. Do not stir again and be careful not to disturb the crust as you strain off the consommé – it's as simple as that!

radish consommé
with soy and shiitake mushrooms

SERVES 6–8

3 bunches of radishes, well trimmed and roughly chopped ●

1 heaped teaspoon shredded ginger root ●

1 tablespoon dark soy sauce ●

2³/₄ cups (1¹/₄ pints) chicken broth ●

1¹/₂ cups (4 oz.) shiitake mushrooms, stalks discarded and cut into fine strips ●

Handful of fresh cilantro leaves ●

Place the radishes in a large saucepan with the ginger, soy and broth and bring to a boil.

Remove the soup from the heat and puree in a food processor or with a hand held blender, then pass through a fine sieve lined with cheesecloth.

Return the soup to a clean saucepan and reheat gently. Season to taste. Divide the mushrooms among the warmed consommé cups or wide-rimmed bowls and scatter the cilantro on top. Ladle over the hot consommé and serve at once.

Coconut milk, one of my favorite ingredients, makes a fantastic creamy base for all the vegetables in this Asian-style soup. The curry powder also helps towards the excellent final flavor. Just make sure you use a fresh, good-quality curry powder and not one that has been stuck in the back of the cupboard for the last six months!

coconut and curry emulsion

SERVES 4

2 tablespoons olive oil

2-inch piece (1 oz.) freshly grated ginger root ●

1 shallot, finely chopped ●

¼ red onion, finely chopped ●

1 small carrot, diced ●

1½ tablespoons (1 oz.) curry powder ●

2 x 14 oz. cans coconut milk ●

Heat the olive oil in a large saucepan. Add the ginger, shallots, red onion and carrot and sauté for about 5 minutes until softened but not colored, stirring occasionally.

Add the curry powder to the saucepan and cook for another 2–3 minutes, stirring constantly. Pour in 5 tablespoons (3 fl.oz.) of water and bring to a boil, then add the coconut milk and just warm through.

Puree the soup in batches in a food processor or with a hand-held blender. Return to a clean saucepan and season to taste. Reheat gently, then ladle into warmed serving bowls and serve at once.

take 6
ingredients | soups

This soup is about as instant as you are ever going to get. It is good served both hot and cold, and the addition of the mint gives it a wonderful zing. You don't have to use fresh peas, as frozen work perfectly well when they are not in season, but freshly podded peas have a particular sweetness that I just love.

pea and mint soup with sour cream

SERVES 4

2 shallots, chopped ●

1½ cups (1 lb.) shelled ●
fresh peas

1½ tablespoons (1 oz.) ●
chopped fresh thyme

5 tablespoons (3 fl.oz.) ●
light cream

1½ tablespoons (1 oz.) fresh ●
mint leaves, finely shredded,
plus a few whole leaves
to garnish

⅔ cup (1¼ pints) sour cream ●

Bring 3¾ cups (1½ pints) of water to a boil in a saucepan and then add the shallots, peas, thyme and thin cream. Simmer gently for 8–10 minutes until the peas are completely tender and season to taste.

Puree the soup in batches in a food processor or with a hand-held blender, and then push through a fine sieve for a smoother, more velvety finish, if liked.

If serving warm, pour back into a clean saucepan, add the mint and season to taste. Reheat gently. Otherwise, just stir in the mint and chill for at least 2 hours. Ladle into wide-rimmed bowls and swirl the sour cream into each serving. Garnish with a few mint leaves and sprinkle with black pepper to serve.

take 6
ingredients | soups

sauvignon blanc soup
with smoked salmon

SERVES 4

2 cups (18 fl.oz.) fish broth ●

1 cup (9 fl.oz.) light cream ●

1 cup (9 fl.oz.) Sauvignon blanc ●

5 egg yolks ●

Good pinch of freshly ●
shredded nutmeg

4 smoked salmon slices ●

Place the fish broth in a heavy saucepan with the cream, Sauvignon blanc, egg yolks and enough nutmeg to taste. Whisk until well combined, then bring to a gentle simmer and continue to cook, whisking continuously until the soup has slightly thickened and reached a soup-like consistency. Remove from the heat and season to taste.

Cut the salmon into strips and divide between four warmed wide-rimmed bowls. Ladle over the soup and add a sprinkling of black pepper and nutmeg to serve.

lemon soup

SERVES 8–10

3 large eggs ●

finely grated rind and juice of ●
3 lemons

6¼ cups (2½ pints) ●
chicken broth

6 oz. coarse semolina ●

1 tablespoon chopped fresh ●
flat-leaf parsley

Break the eggs into a large heatproof bowl and stir in the lemon juice. Set aside.

Place the broth in a large saucepan with the lemon rind and bring to a boil, then reduce the heat and simmer for 5 minutes to allow the flavors to combine.

Stir the semolina into the egg and lemon juice mixture, then slowly pour over the stock, whisking to combine.

Pour the broth mixture back into the saucepan and season to taste, then just heat through. Ladle the soup into bowls and garnish with the parsley to serve.

take **6**
ingredients | soups

Sauvignon blanc soup with smoked salmon

salads

I just love this simple salad. Black pudding is so cheap – buy from a good butcher and be careful not to overcook it as it tends to lose its succulence quite easily. Each portion of salad is served with a poached egg on top – these are so easy to prepare in advance, then you just slip them back into hot salted water when you are ready to serve.

frisée, pancetta,
black pudding and poached egg salad

SERVES 4

$2/3$ cup ($1/4$ pint) olive oil

2 tablespoons balsamic vinegar ●
(12 year old)

1 small shallot, ●
roughly chopped

4 oz. piece of pancetta ●
(Italian streaky bacon)

4 oz. black pudding ●

1 large head frisée ●
(curly) lettuce

To make the balsamic dressing, place $1/2$ cup of the olive oil in a food processor or liquidizer with the balsamic vinegar and shallot. Season to taste and blend until smooth. Pour into a screw-topped bottle and chill until ready to use – you wont need all of this to dress the salad, but it will keep perfectly well for up to three to four days in the fridge.

Heat a skillet. Cut the pancetta into $1/4$-inch cubes. Add a tablespoon of the oil to the pan and then tip in the pancetta. Stir-fry for 2–3 minutes until lightly golden. Drain on paper towels.

Cut the black pudding into four even-sized slices and then cut each one into six triangles. Wipe out the skillet, add the remaining oil and fry the black pudding triangles for a minute or so, turning once until sizzling. Drain on paper towels.

Meanwhile, poach the eggs. Pour $1^{1}/_{2}$-inch of boiling water into a skillet and place over a low heat – the water should show a few bubbles on the base of the skillet but no more. Carefully break in the eggs and cook for 3 minutes, basting the tops of the eggs with a little of the hot water as they cook. Remove with a slotted spoon and drain briefly on paper towels.

Strip back the head of frisée lettuce, leaving mainly the light green heart leaves and then separate out the leaves. Wash well and dry in a salad spinner or with plenty of paper towels. Place in a bowl and pour in enough of the balsamic dressing to just lightly coat, then season and toss to combine.

Arrange the dressed lettuce in wide-rimmed bowls and scatter over the pancetta and black pudding. Place a poached egg on top of each one and season to taste. Serve immediately.

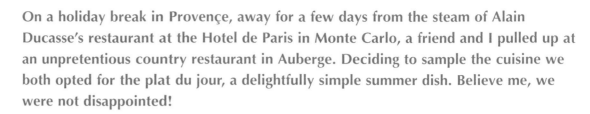

On a holiday break in Provençe, away for a few days from the steam of Alain Ducasse's restaurant at the Hotel de Paris in Monte Carlo, a friend and I pulled up at an unpretentious country restaurant in Auberge. Deciding to sample the cuisine we both opted for the plat du jour, a delightfully simple summer dish. Believe me, we were not disappointed!

spicy chicken salad

with sun-blushed tomatoes

SERVES 4

1 tablespoon all-purpose flour ●

1 tablespoon five-spice powder ●

2 chicken breast fillets ●

5 tablespoons olive oil

5 oz. packet of mixed herb ●
salad

1 cup (4 oz.) sun-blushed ●
tomatoes

1 cup (4 oz.) black olives ●
(good quality)

Heat a non-stick skillet. Place the flour and five-spice powder in a shallow dish and season generously. Mix thoroughly. Cut the chicken breasts into 3/4-inch strips and toss in the flour mixture to coat, shaking off any excess. Add two tablespoons of the olive oil to the pan and then add the chicken strips. Gently fry for about 4 minutes, turning once until crispy and golden brown.

Place the salad leaves in a bowl and add enough of the remaining oil to just barely coat the leaves and then season generously. Toss to coat. Arrange the sun-blushed tomatoes and olives in wide-rimmed bowls. Place the crispy chicken on top, add the salad leaves and finally drizzle over the rest of the oil to serve.

take 6
ingredients | salads

This is one of my barbecue party staples as it's a classy-looking salad that tastes great – and all of the work is done ahead of serving. Make the cous cous in advance, and either serve cold or reheat in the oven, or even better, in a microwave. Stir in the yellow pesto just before serving or the cous cous will loose some of its texture. It goes great with almost anything, but is especially good with charbroiled oily fish, such as sardines or mackerel.

warm cous cous salad

with yellow pesto

SERVES 4

1 large yellow bell pepper ●

6 tablespoons olive oil

1 tablespoon (¹/₂ oz.) freshly ●
shredded Parmesan

1¹/₄ cups (¹/₂ pint) chicken or ●
vegetable broth

³/₄ tablespoon (¹/₂ oz.) ●
unsalted butter

1¹/₂ cups (9 oz.) cous cous ●

2 tablespoons snipped ●
fresh chives

Preheat the broiler until very hot. To make the pesto, cut the bell pepper in half and remove the pips, stalk and inner membrane. Sprinkle a roasting pan with sea salt and a little olive oil. Place the bell pepper cut side down in the pan and drizzle another tablespoon of oil on top. Place under the broiler and cook for about 10 minutes or until the skin is blackened and blistered.

Transfer the pepper halves to a bowl with tongs and cover with plastic wrap – this will help the skins to steam off. Leave to cool completely, then peel away and discard the skins. Roughly chop the pepper flesh and place in a food processor or liquidizer and blend to a puree. Add the Parmesan and the remaining olive oil and blend again until smooth. Season to taste.

Place the broth in a saucepan and add the butter, then season to taste and bring to a simmer. Place the cous cous in a large heatproof bowl and then pour over the broth mixture. Cover with plastic wrap or aluminum foil and set aside for 5 minutes, then using a fork fluff up the grains so that they separate. Stir in the yellow bell pepper pesto and spoon into wide-rimmed bowls. Scatter over the chives and serve warm or cold.

take 6
ingredients | salads

Tuna from the store-cupboard often comes to our rescue when we want a quick ingredient, and once you've tasted these stuffed bell peppers you'll agree that this is one of the best ideas yet. Be sure to accompany this salad with lots of warm crusty bread for mopping up all the delicious juices.

salad with tuna-stuffed bell pepper

SERVES 4

2 large yellow bell peppers ●

1 tablespoon olive oil

6½ oz. can of tuna in ●
olive oil, drained

1 tablespoon rinsed, ●
chopped capers

3–4 tablespoons mayonnaise ●
(preferably home-made)

7 oz. bag of mixed salad leaves ●

6 tablespoons French dressing ●
(preferably home-made)

Preheat the oven to 350°F. Brush the bell peppers with the olive oil and arrange on a baking sheet. Roast for 8–10 minutes until the skins are slightly blistered and the bell peppers are tender, but still holding their shape.

Transfer the bell peppers to a large bowl, cover with plastic wrap and leave to cool completely – this will help steam the skins off. Carefully peel away the skins, then cut each bell pepper in half and remove the stalks and inner membrane.

Finely chop the tuna, then transfer to a bowl and add the capers and season to taste. Mix in enough of the mayonnaise to bind and then fill the bell pepper halves – this will also help them to keep their shape.

Place the salad leaves in a bowl, season and pour in half of the dressing, tossing to coat. Arrange on serving plates and place a stuffed bell pepper on top of each one. Drizzle the remaining dressing over the stuffed pepper halves and serve immediately.

take 6
ingredients | salads

This was devised one Sunday lunchtime when I realized I didn't have enough roast beef to go around. It is a wonderful dish, full of complementing flavors and textures. I like to use mescluna salad leaves for the salad base but a mixture of wild arugula, watercress and baby spinach leaves would also work well. Raspberry-infused olive oil is now available in speciality food stores and deli's. However, if you have any problems finding it, use a good-quality olive oil and add a dash of raspberry vinegar.

traffic jam roast beef

and blue cheese salad

SERVES 4

1 lb. sirloin or filet mignon ● (well hung)

2 tablespoons olive oil

5 cups (1 lb.) mixed salad ●

16 cherry tomatoes, halved ●

1/2 red onion, thinly sliced ●

1 1/2 cups (8 oz.) blue cheese, ● crumbled (such as Gorgonzola, Roquefort or Cashel Blue)

5 tablespoons (3 fl.oz.) ● raspberry-infused olive oil (see above)

Preheat the oven to 450°F. Heat an ovenproof skillet until very hot. Season the beef. Add the olive oil to the skillet and add the beef, then brown well on all sides. Remove from the heat, drain off any excess oil and then place the beef in the oven for 5 minutes. Remove from the oven and leave to stand in a warm place until the beef has relaxed. This will take at least 30 minutes, but you could leave the beef to stand for up to 2 hours, provided it's not in too hot a place.

When the beef has rested and you are ready to serve transfer it on to a carving board. Use a very sharp carving knife to cut it into very thin slices. Arrange the salad leaves in wide-rimmed bowls, then fold the slices of beef into cone shapes and pile them on top of the salad leaves. Scatter over the cherry tomatoes, red onion slices and blue cheese. Add a good drizzle of the raspberry-infused olive oil, then season to taste and serve.

take 6
ingredients | salads

This salad gives loads of flavor for minimum effort and is perfect for lazy, hazy summer days. The fresh zingy flavor of the citrus fruit cuts through the richness of the salmon perfectly. Just be careful not to overcook the salmon; it should be still very moist and pink inside when it is served.

seared fillet of salmon
with new potatoes and citrus salad

SERVES 4

16 small new potatoes, scrubbed clean ●

3 oranges ●

3 lemons ●

About 1/2 cup (4 fl.oz.) olive oil

4 salmon fillets, skinned ●

4 tablespoons chopped fresh cilantro ●

21/2 cups (7 oz.) arugula leaves ●

Place the potatoes in a saucepan of boiling salted water and bring to a boil, then cover, reduce the heat and simmer for 12–15 minutes or until just tender. Drain, allow to cool a little and then cut into slices. Season and drizzle over a little of the olive oil.

Holding one of the oranges over a large bowl to catch the juices, peel and segment discarding all the pith, using a sharp serrated knife. Prepare the remaining oranges and the lemons in the same way. Place the orange and lemon segments in a separate bowl. Add 1/3 cup (3.5.fl oz.) of the olive oil to the juices and whisk together to combine, then season to taste.

Heat a non-stick skillet. Season the salmon fillets. Add the remaining olive oil to the skillet and then add the salmon fillets, presentation side down and cook for 3–4 minutes until well seared and lightly golden. Turn over the fillets and cook for another minute until just tender. Transfer to a plate and keep warm.

Tip the orange and lemon segments into the dressing and then add the cilantro and arugula leaves, tossing to combine. Arrange the salmon fillets on serving plates and place the new potatoes on the side with the arugula salad on top.

take 6
ingredients | salads

pastas and risottos

Piperade is a sauté of vegetables from the Basque region in France into which eggs are normally beaten. Here I am serving it with pasta and a seared tuna steak which I have cooked rare so that it remains moist and succulent in the middle.

seared tuna

with piperade and linguine

SERVES 4

4 tablespoons olive oil

4 shallots, thinly sliced ●

4 garlic cloves, finely chopped ●

2 red and 2 yellow bell peppers, seeded and thinly sliced ●

4 plum tomatoes, peeled, pitted and roughly chopped ●

4 cups (12 oz.) linguine pasta ●

Four x medium (5 oz.) tuna steaks ●

Heat a large heavy saucepan. Add two tablespoons of the olive oil and then tip in the shallots and cook for about 5 minutes or until softened and just beginning to brown at the edges.

Stir the garlic into the shallot mixture and continue to cook for another minute or so, then add the bell peppers, cover and simmer for 10–15 minutes or until the bell peppers are completely tender and softened, stirring occasionally.

Stir the tomatoes into the bell pepper mixture and continue to cook for a further 15 minutes or so, stirring occasionally until most of the moisture from the tomatoes has evaporated and the vegetable stew mixture is fairly dry. Season to taste.

Meanwhile, cook the linguine in a large saucepan of boiling salted water for 8–10 minutes or according to packet instructions, until al dente. Drain and quickly refresh under cold running water, then toss in a tablespoon of the olive oil.

Heat a griddle pan until searing hot. Brush each tuna steak with a little of the remaining oil and season generously, then add to the pan and cook for 1–2 minutes on each side, depending on how rare you like your fish.

Divide the pasta among warmed wide-rimmed bowls and spoon the piperade around the edge. Place a tuna steak on each serving and serve at once.

To make this risotto a little richer you could add a handful of grated Parmesan or a couple of spoonfuls of mascarpone cheese. I also like to garnish it with sprigs of fresh chervils. The key to the success of this risotto is buying fresh sardines that have not been previously frozen. Just check with your fishmonger before buying them.

saffron risotto with
red bell peppers and grilled sardines

SERVES 4

1 red bell pepper ●

About 4 tablespoons olive oil

8 cups (3–3¹/₂ pints) chicken ●
broth (preferably home-made)

2¹/₃ cups (14 oz.) risotto rice ●

good pinch of saffron strands, ●
soaked in a little warm water

12 x (2 oz.) sardine ●
fillets, cleaned

¹/₂ cup (4 fl.oz.) heavy cream, ●
lightly whipped

Cut the bell pepper in half, remove the pips, stalk and inner membrane and dice. Set aside.

Pour the broth into a saucepan and bring to a gentle simmer. Heat a heavy saucepan. Add two tablespoons of the olive oil and then add the rice and saffron mixture, then cook for 30 seconds to 1 minute, stirring until the rice has become nutty and perfumed.

Add a ladleful of the simmering broth to the rice, stirring continuously until all the liquid has been absorbed. Continue adding ladlefuls of the broth, stirring all the time and making sure that the last addition has been almost absorbed before adding the next – the whole process takes 18–20 minutes – until the rice is tender, but still *al dente*.

Meanwhile, heat the broiler. Cut the heads off the sardines and then fillet them, leaving them attached at the tail end. Drizzle a little of the remaining oil on a baking sheet and arrange the sardines on top. Season generously and drizzle over the remaining olive oil. Broil for 1–2 minutes on each side until crisp and lightly golden.

Taste the rice, it should be just cooked, then stir in the cream and reserved red bell pepper dice. Season to taste. Ladle the risotto into warmed wide-rimmed bowls and arrange the grilled sardines on top. Serve at once.

take 6
ingredients | pastas and
risottos

Pickled goat cheese balls are now becoming fashionable and can be bought in most good cheese shops. If you want to make them yourself, simply roll a soft, fresh goat cheese into small balls, about the size of chocolate truffles, and place in a bowl. Add a few pink peppercorns and a little Champagne vinegar to taste, then pour over enough olive oil to cover. Cover with plastic wrap and chill for at least 12 hours or up to 2 days, before using as described below.

beet risotto with pickled
goat cheese and charred chicken livers

SERVES 4

1 beet, peeled and cut into dice ●

About 5 cups (2 pints) chicken broth ●
(preferably home-made)

3 tablespoons olive oil

1¹/₄ cups (7 oz.) risotto rice ●

6 oz. fresh chicken livers, trimmed ●
and cut into ¹/₂-inch slices

¹/₃ cup (3¹/₂ fl.oz.) heavy cream, ●
lightly whipped

2 oz. small goat cheese balls, ●
pickled (see above)

Place the beet in a saucepan and pour in ²/₃ cup (¹/₄ pint) of broth and bring to a boil, then simmer gently for about 15 minutes or until the beet is completely tender. Drain, reserving the liquid and place the cooked beet dice in a food processor or liquidizer. Blend briefly, then pour in enough of the reserved liquid to make a smooth puree – you'll need ¹/₂ cup (4 fl.oz.) in total. Pass through a fine strainer lined with cheesecloth for a smoother finish.

Pour the remaining broth into a saucepan and bring to a gentle simmer. Heat a heavy saucepan. Add two tablespoons of the olive oil and then add the rice, then cook for 30 seconds to 1 minute, stirring until nutty and perfumed.

Add a ladleful of the simmering broth to the rice, stirring continuously until all the liquid has been absorbed. Continue adding ladlefuls of the broth, stirring all the time and making sure that the last addition has been almost absorbed before adding the next – the whole process takes 18–20 minutes – until the rice is tender but still *al dente*.

Meanwhile, heat a non-stick skillet. Season the chicken livers. Add the remaining two tablespoons of olive oil to the skillet and then add the chicken livers. Cook for 2-3 minutes, turning once, until sizzling and golden brown, but still pink in the middle. Taste the rice, it should be just cooked, then stir in the cream and the beet puree and season to taste. Ladle the risotto into warmed wide-rimmed bowls and scatter over the pickled goat cheeses, breaking them up as you go. Arrange the chicken livers in a small mound on top and serve at once.

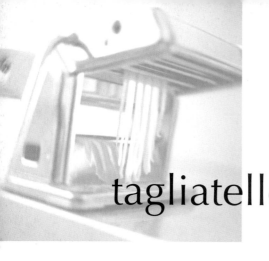

Chicken legs are not only cheaper than breasts, but they can be much tastier in my opinion. The secret is the slow cooking, which would leave a breast fillet dry and tasteless. When using legs you end up with crispy skin and succulent, well-flavored flesh – perfect for this type of pasta dish.

tagliatelle with roasted chicken leg, mushrooms and chile

SERVES 4

8 chicken legs (preferably free-range)

About 2 tablespoons olive oil

4$^{1}/_{2}$ cups (14 oz.) fresh tagliatelle (good quality)

6 shallots, finely chopped

$^{1}/_{2}$ red chile, pitted and finely chopped

3$^{1}/_{2}$ cups (11 oz.) shiitake mushrooms, sliced

4 tablespoons chopped fresh cilantro

Preheat the oven to 350°F. Place the chicken legs in a roasting pan and drizzle with a little olive oil. Season and roast for 20–30 minutes, depending on the size of the legs, until just tender and cooked through.

Increase the oven temperature to 400°F and roast the chicken legs for another 10 minutes or until the skin is crisp and golden brown.

Meanwhile, cook the tagliatelle in a large saucepan of boiling salted water for 2 minutes until *al dente*. Drain and quickly refresh under cold running water.

Heat the remaining tablespoon of olive oil in a large non-stick skillet and add the shallots. Cook for 1 minute, stirring, then add the chile and shiitake mushrooms. Increase the heat and cook for a further 2 minutes, stirring constantly.

Mix the tagliatelle into the mushroom mixture with most of the cilantro, reserving some for garnish. Season to taste. Divide the pasta between warmed wide-rimmed bowls and arrange two chicken legs on top of each serving. Garnish with the remaining cilantro and serve at once.

take 6 ingredients | pastas and risottos

Prosciutto is the classic Italian ham that traditionally came from pigs fattened on a diet of parsnips. In fact, most are now fed a diet of whey left over from making the local cheese, Parmesan. The ham is then dry-cured under weights and matured for at least a year, before being sold.

tomato and basil risotto
with prosciutto and bread croutons

SERVES 4

5 tablespoons olive oil

4 plum tomatoes, peeled, pitted and chopped

Handful (1 oz.) fresh basil leaves, shredded

1 Italian baguette, cut into croutons

2¹/₃ cups (14 oz.) risotto rice

¹/₃ cup (3¹/₂ fl.oz.) light cream

8 oz. Italian prosciutto, thinly sliced

Preheat the broiler. Heat a tablespoon of the olive oil in a non-stick skillet. Add the tomatoes and season generously. Cook gently for 5–10 minutes until you have achieved a rich pulp, stirring occasionally. Remove from the heat and stir in the basil. Set aside.

Place the croutons on a large baking sheet and drizzle over about two tablespoons of the olive oil. Toast under the broiler until crispy and golden brown, turning occasionally.

Pour 7¹/₂ cups (3 pints) of water into a saucepan and bring to a gentle simmer. Heat a heavy saucepan. Add the remaining two tablespoons of olive oil and then add the rice. Cook for 30 seconds to 1 minute, stirring until the oil has been absorbed and the rice has become translucent.

Add a ladleful of the simmering water to the pan, stirring continuously until all the liquid has been absorbed. Continue adding ladlefuls of the water, stirring all the time and making sure that the last addition has been almost absorbed before adding the next – the whole process takes about 18–20 minutes – until the rice is tender but still *al dente*. Taste the rice, it should be just cooked, then stir in the reserved tomato pulp, and the cream, then season to taste. Divide the risotto between warmed wide-rimmed bowls and arrange the prosciutto on top. Scatter over the croutons to serve.

The secret with this sauce is not to overcook it, and there's usually enough residual heat in the pan to cook the egg and cream mixture off the stove. You could replace the bacon with pancetta (Italian thick-sliced bacon) for a more authentic flavor. This should take no more that 15 minutes from start to finish to prepare, and is great served with a light arugula salad and a decent glass of wine.

pasta carbonara

SERVES 4–6

4 cups (1 lb.) fettucine or rigatoni pasta ●

3 tablespoons olive oil

4 shallots, chopped ●

4 oz. thick-sliced bacon, chopped ●

3 egg yolks ●

1¹/₃ cups (12 fl.oz.) heavy cream ●

1³/₄ cups (4 oz.) freshly shredded Parmesan ●

Bring a large saucepan of salted water to a boil. Add the fettucine or rigatoni, stir once, and cook for 4–10 minutes, depending on packet instructions, until *al dente*. Drain and refresh briefly under cold running water, then set aside.

Heat a large heavy skillet. Add the olive oil and then tip in the shallots and sauté for 1 minute. Add the bacon and continue to cook for 3–5 minutes until crisp. Remove from the heat.

Whisk the egg yolks in a bowl with the cream until frothy, then beat in ²/₃ cup (1¹/₂ oz.) of the Parmesan. Season to taste.

Add the pasta to the shallot and bacon mixture. Return the skillet to a low heat and allow to just warm through, stirring to ensure that everything is well combined. Remove from the heat, then quickly pour in the cream mixture, tossing well to coat. The residual heat should start to cook the sauce – if not, stir over a very gentle heat for a second or two to cook a bit more. Divide the pasta between warmed wide-rimmed bowls and garnish with the remaining Parmesan. Serve at once.

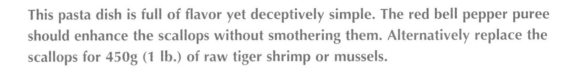

This pasta dish is full of flavor yet deceptively simple. The red bell pepper puree should enhance the scallops without smothering them. Alternatively replace the scallops for 450g (1 lb.) of raw tiger shrimp or mussels.

roasted scallops with shiitake mushrooms, red bell pepper and penne

SERVES 4

- 5 red bell peppers
- 1/2 cup (4 fl.oz.) olive oil
- 3 cups (12 oz.) penne pasta
- 12 large scallops, cleaned
- 3 cups (9 oz.) shiitake mushrooms, sliced
- 1 garlic clove, crushed
- 1/2 red chile, pitted and finely chopped

Preheat the broiler until very hot. Cut four of the bell peppers in half and remove the pips, stalk and inner membrane. Sprinkle a roasting pan with sea salt and a tablespoon of the olive oil. Place the bell peppers cut side down in the pan and drizzle another tablespoon of the olive oil. Grill for about 10 minutes or until the skins are blackened and blistered.

Transfer the bell pepper halves to a bowl with tongs and cover with plastic wrap – this will help the skins to steam off. Leave to cool, then peel away the skins and discard. Roughly chop the bell pepper flesh and place in a food processor or liquidizer. Whizz to blend whilst pouring about four tablespoons of the olive oil in through the feeder tube to make a smooth puree – you'll need about 1 cup (9 fl.oz.) in total. Season and set aside.

Meanwhile, cook the penne in a large saucepan of boiling salted water for 8–10 minutes, or according to packet instructions, until *al dente*. Pat the scallops dry with paper towels. Detach the roes (corals) and discard or save them for another dish; then carefully cut away the small moon-shaped muscle as it will become very tough when cooked, then cut each one in half again to give round, disc shapes. Cut the remaining bell pepper in half and remove the pips, then thinly slice. Set aside. Pour the red bell pepper puree into a small saucepan and just warm through, stirring occasionally.

Heat a wok until searing hot. Add the remaining two tablespoons of olive oil, then add the scallops and stir-fry for 30 seconds until just sealed. Tip in the shiitake mushrooms and continue to stir-fry whilst adding the garlic, chile and reserved sliced red bell pepper in this order. Remove from the heat, season to taste and pour over the warmed red bell pepper puree. Drain the penne and then stir into the scallop mixture until just combined. Divide between warmed wide-rimmed bowls and scatter over some chopped fresh cilantro to serve, if liked.

take 6
ingredients | pastas and risottos

This has to be the ultimate risotto! When ceps are in season there is nothing else like it. However, if you find them difficult to get hold of use reconstituted dried porcini mushrooms for that authentic flavor and combine them with a selection of mixed wild mushrooms which are now readily available. I tend to find this particular risotto quite rich (not to mention expensive to make) so you might want to consider smaller portions than you normally would...

cep risotto

with parmesan and mascarpone

SERVES 2–4

About 4 cups (1³/4 pints) chicken broth (preferably home-made) ●

3 tablespoons olive oil

3¹/2 cups (11 oz.) cep ● mushrooms, wiped clean, trimmed and sliced

1¹/4 cups (7 oz.) risotto rice ●

¹/3 cup (³/4 stick) ● unsalted butter

2 cups (5 oz.) freshly ● shredded Parmesan

4 tablespoons (2 oz.) ● mascarpone cheese

Pour the broth into a saucepan and bring to a gentle simmer. Heat a heavy saucepan. Add two tablespoons of the olive oil and then tip in half of the ceps and sauté for 3–4 minutes until just tender. Add the rice, then cook for 30 seconds to 1 minute, stirring until the rice has become nutty and perfumed.

Add a ladleful of the simmering broth to the rice, stirring continuously until all the liquid has been absorbed. Continue adding ladlefuls of the stock, stirring all the time and making sure that the last addition has been almost absorbed before adding the next – the whole process takes 18–20 minutes – until the rice is tender but still *al dente*.

Meanwhile, heat a non-stick skillet. Add the remaining tablespoon of oil and a knob of the butter and sauté the remaining ceps for about 5 minutes until tender. Season to taste. Taste the rice, it should be just cooked, then stir in the Parmesan, mascarpone cheese and remaining butter. Season to taste. Ladle the risotto into warmed wide-rimmed bowls and arrange a small mound of the sautéed ceps on top of each one. Serve at once.

For me, there's not much that can beat this creamy risotto, especially as it's served with juicy tiger shrimp. The trick of a good risotto is to add the broth little by little, allowing the liquid to be almost completely absorbed before adding the next ladleful.

red bell pepper risotto

with pan-fried tiger shrimp

SERVES 4

4 red bell peppers ●

9 tablespoons olive oil

8 cups (3–3½ pints) chicken ● broth (preferably home-made)

2½ cups (14 oz.) risotto rice ●

½ cup (3½ fl. oz.) heavy cream ●

1⅓ cups (4 oz.) freshly ● shredded Parmesan

20 raw tiger shrimp, ● peeled and cleaned

Preheat the broiler until very hot. Cut the bell peppers in half and remove the pips, stalk and inner membrane. Sprinkle a roasting pan with sea salt and a tablespoon of the olive oil. Place the bell peppers cut side down in the pan and drizzle another tablespoon of the olive oil. Broil for about 10 minutes or until the skins are blackened and blistered.

Transfer the bell pepper halves to a bowl and cover with plastic wrap – this will help the skins to steam off. Leave to cool, then peel away the skins and discard. Roughly chop the bell pepper flesh and place in a food processor or liquidizer. Whizz to blend whilst pouring four tablespoons of the remaining oil in through the feeder tube to make a smooth puree – you'll need about 1 cup (9 fl.oz.) in total. Transfer to a jug and cover with plasic wrap. Chill until ready to use.

Pour the broth into a saucepan and bring to a gentle simmer. Heat a heavy saucepan. Add two tablespoons of the olive oil and then add the rice. Cook for 30 seconds to 1 minute, stirring until the oil has been absorbed and the rice has become translucent.

Add a ladleful of the simmering broth to the rice, stirring continuously until all the liquid has been absorbed. Continue adding ladlefuls of the stock, stirring all the time and making sure that the last addition has been almost absorbed before adding the next. After about 12 minutes when the rice is beginning to soften, add the red bell pepper puree and cook for a few minutes more, stirring continuously.

Meanwhile, heat a non-stick skillet. Taste the rice, it should be just cooked – *al dente*, stir in the cream and Parmesan. Season to taste. Add the remaining tablespoon of the olive oil, then add the shrimp and cook for a minute or so until they turn pink. Ladle the risotto into warmed wide-rimmed bowls and arrange five of the shrimp on top of each one. Garnish with lightly dressed arugula leaves, and serve immediately.

take 6
ingredients | pastas and risottos

This pasta dish is easy to make and perfect for a mid-week dinner party (because the sauce can be made well in advance and just stirred into the pasta with the feta at the last minute). It makes a nice change from your average tomato-flavored sauce, but should only be made when ripe plum tomatoes are available.

penne with tomato and vodka sauce

SERVES 4–6

½ cup (4 fl.oz.) olive oil

10 plum tomatoes, peeled, pitted and diced

4 cups (1 lb.) penne pasta

4 garlic cloves, finely chopped

¾ cup (4 oz.) black olives (good quality)

2 cups (18 fl.oz.) vodka

1½ cups (8 oz.) feta cheese, crumbled

To prepare the stewed tomatoes, heat a heavy saucepan, then add two tablespoons of the olive oil before adding half of the plum tomatoes. Season and simmer gently for 10–15 minutes until all the liquid has evaporated and the tomato stew is quite dry. Season to taste and allow to cool. Set aside.

Bring a large saucepan of salted water to a boil. Add the penne, stir once and cook for 6–10 minutes, or according to packet instructions, until *al dente*. Drain and refresh briefly under cold running water, then set aside.

Heat a large heavy sauté skillet until hot. Add the remaining six tablespoons of the olive oil and once heated, tip in the garlic, stirring vigorously to make sure that it does not burn. When it is golden brown, add the remaining plum tomatoes and sauté for another 2 minutes.

Add the olives to the skillet, stir and season to taste. Pour in the vodka and allow to reduce until all the alcohol has evaporated. Add the reserved stewed tomatoes and simmer gently for 6–8 minutes or until the sauce has thickened, stirring occasionally.

Add the penne to the skillet with the tomato and vodka sauce and simmer until just warmed through, stirring constantly to ensure that the penne gets evenly coated. Remove from the heat and stir in the feta cheese, then divide between warmed wide-rimmed bowls. Serve immediately.

take 6
ingredients | pastas and risottos

fish and shellfish

The slightly smoky flavors of salmon seared at high temperatures blend well with the sweetness of the bell peppers and the crunchiness of the fennel. Try not to overcook your salmon. Ideally it should be served slightly pink in the middle.

pan-fried salmon with salad of fennel, sweet red bell pepper and dill

SERVES 4

4 red bell peppers ●

1 fennel bulb ●

Large handful (1 oz.) chopped ●
fresh dill

Juice of 1 lemon ●

About ⅔ cup (¼ pint) ●
extra virgin olive oil

4 x medium (6 oz.) salmon ●
fillets, unskinned

To make the salad, blanch the red bell peppers for a minute or two in a saucepan of boiling water. Remove from the heat and plunge into a bowl of cold water. Cut each bell pepper in half, remove the core and pips, then cut into thin slices. Pat dry with paper towels to remove excess moisture.

Remove the feathery tips and outer leaves from the fennel and then using a very sharp knife cut into wafer-thin slices. Place in a bowl with the pepper slices, dill, lemon juice and enough of the olive oil to bind. Season to taste.

Heat a heavy skillet. Season the salmon fillets. Add two tablespoons of oil to the pan and then add the salmon, skin side down. Cook over a medium heat for 4–5 minutes until the skin is crisp and golden brown, then turn over and cook for another minute or two until just cooked through.

Spoon the fennel salad into the center of wide-rimmed bowls and arrange the salmon on top. Serve immediately with a spoonful of sour cream, if liked.

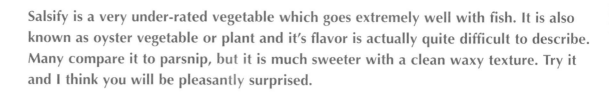

Salsify is a very under-rated vegetable which goes extremely well with fish. It is also known as oyster vegetable or plant and it's flavor is actually quite difficult to describe. Many compare it to parsnip, but it is much sweeter with a clean waxy texture. Try it and I think you will be pleasantly surprised.

pan-roasted sea bass with spinach,
salsify and wholegrain mustard

SERVES 4

4¹/₂ oz. (about a cup) salsify, peeled and covered in acidulated water ●

1 tablespoon all-purpose flour ●

4 x medium (6 oz.) sea bass fillets, unskinned ●

3 tablespoons olive oil

5 cups (8 oz.) fresh baby spinach ●

1 cup (9 fl.oz.) heavy cream ●

¹/₂ cup (4 oz.) wholegrain mustard (preferably Pommery) ●

Place the salsify in a saucepan of boiling water with the flour. Bring to a boil, then reduce the heat and simmer for about 30 minutes or until *al dente*. Drain and set aside.

Heat a non-stick skillet. Season the sea bass fillets. Add two tablespoons of the olive oil and cook the sea bass skin-side down for 2–3 minutes until the skin is crisp and golden brown, then turn over and cook for another minute or two until it is just cooked through.

Meanwhile, heat a separate saucepan. Add the remaining tablespoon of the olive oil and tip in the spinach. Sauté the spinach for a minute or so until it has just wilted, then season to taste.

Place the cream in a saucepan with the mustard and just warm through. Add the blanched salsify and simmer gently until heated through, stirring occasionally. Season to taste.

Arrange the spinach in warmed wide-rimmed serving bowls and place the sea bass on top. Garnish with the salsify and spoon over any remaining cream sauce to serve.

take 6
ingredients | fish and
shellfish

Real balsamic vinegar is made in the area around Modena in Italy where the extremes of temperatures and climate contribute to the maturing process. It is actually the boiled and concentrated juice of local trebbiano grapes that has been aged in a series of barrels of decreasing size and different woods which gives it a slightly syrupy texture and a rich, deep mahogany color. Only buy the genuine article (aceto balsamico tradizionale di Modena) which is strictly controlled by law; it must be aged for at least 12 years. Vinegar aged 20 years or more is called stravecchio.

seared scallops with broad beans
and mint puree with aged balsamic

SERVES 4

- 1 cup (9 fl.oz.) balsamic vinegar (12 year old)

- 16 large scallops, cleaned

- 8 oz. podded fava beans

- 4 tablespoons sour cream

- 2 tablespoons chopped fresh mint

- Grated rind and juice of 1 lemon

- About 1 tablespoon olive oil

Place the balsamic vinegar in a heavy saucepan and simmer for 6–8 minutes until slightly reduced and syrupy. Allow to cool and then pour into a squeezy plastic bottle. The remainder of this can be used for other dishes.

Pat the scallops dry with paper towels. Detach the roes (corals) and discard or save them for another dish; then carefully cut away the small moon-shaped muscle as it will become very tough when cooked.

Blanch the beans in a saucepan of boiling water for 30 seconds, then drain and refresh. Peel away the outer skins and discard them. Return the beans to the saucepan with a tablespoon of water. Stir in the sour cream, mint and lemon rind and juice. Season and just warm through, then tip into a food processor or liquidizer and blend to a puree. Season to taste.

Meanwhile, heat a large skillet until it is quite hot. Season the scallops. Add a thin film of olive oil to the skillet and then add the scallops. Sear for a minute or so on each side until just tender and slightly caramelized.

Spoon the bean puree into the center of warmed wide-rimmed bowls and arrange the scallops around the edge. Drizzle over some of the balsamic syrup and serve immediately.

take 6
ingredients | fish and shellfish

Red snapper is an exotic fish that is now widely available – expect a glossy, firm fish with a delicate flavor, so keep things as simple and panic free as possible. I like to serve this with buttered couscous which I find actually benefits from being made the day before and reheated.

pan-roasted red snapper with
basil puree and grilled yellow bell peppers

SERVES 4

Large handful (1 oz.) fresh basil leaves ●

4 garlic cloves, peeled ●

1/3 cup (1 oz.) freshly shredded Parmesan ●

1 cup (9 fl.oz.) olive oil

6 yellow bell peppers ●

4 x medium (6 oz.) red snapper fillets, unskinned ●

Plunge the basil into a saucepan of boiling water and blanch for 2–3 seconds, then plunge into a bowl of ice-cold water – this will help to retain the color. Drain the basil and gently pat dry with paper towels, then place in a food processor or liquidizer. Add the garlic, Parmesan and 3/4 cup (7 fl.oz.) of olive oil and blend to a puree. Season to taste and transfer to a bottle with a lid. Chill until ready to use.

Preheat the broiler. Cut each bell pepper into quarters, then remove the cores and pips. Toss in two tablespoons of the olive oil and then arrange on the broiler rack. Season the bell peppers and broil for about 10 minutes until softened and lightly charred, turning occasionally.

Meanwhile, heat a large skillet until very hot. Cut a few shallow slashes in the skin of each red snapper fillet to help prevent them from curling during cooking. Add the remaining olive oil to the skillet and then add the red snapper fillets, skin-side down. Cook for 4–5 minutes, until the skin is crisp and lightly golden, then turn over and cook for another minute or so until tender. Transfer to a baking sheet, season to taste and keep warm.

Shake the basil dressing in the bottle until well combined, then spoon into the bottom of warmed serving plates. Arrange the red snapper fillets on top and garnish with the grilled yellow bell peppers. Serve immediately with buttered couscous and a mixed leaf salad, if liked.

The firm flesh and sturdy flavor of the monkfish allow for robust treatment and the rich flavor of the pancetta which I've used in this dish. Here the fish fillets are wrapped in delicate thin slices of pancetta before being steamed and roasted in the oven until the pancetta is crispy. They are then sliced and served with rich chive potatoes, which balance the saltiness of the pancetta perfectly.

loin of monkfish wrapped in
pancetta with chive potatoes

SERVES 4

1 lb. (about 3 medium) waxy potatoes, peeled and cut into small dice ●

2/3 cup (1/4 pint) heavy cream ●

1 garlic clove, crushed ●

4 x medium (5 oz.) monkfish loin, well trimmed ●

12–16 slices wafer-thin pancetta ●

2 tablespoons snipped fresh chives, plus extra whole ones to garnish ●

Preheat the oven to 400°F. Cook the potatoes in a covered saucepan of boiling salted water for 5–10 minutes until tender. Place the cream and garlic in a small saucepan and simmer until reduced by half.

Meanwhile, roll each piece of the monkfish in pancetta so that it is completely covered and then wrap tightly in plastic wrap to help keep the shape. Place in a steamer and cook for 5 minutes, then quickly remove the plastic wrap and place in a roasting pan. Roast for 5–10 minutes or until the monkfish is just tender and the pancetta is crispy. Leave to rest for a minute or two in a warm place.

Drain the potatoes and return to the saucepan to dry out for a minute or so, then pour in the reduced cream and add the chives. Season to taste. Carefully fold the flavorings into the potatoes, being careful not to break them up.

Cut each piece of monkfish into medallions on the diagonal. Spoon the potatoes into warmed wide-rimmed bowls. Arrange the monkfish medallions on top and garnish with some whole chives. Serve immediately.

seared tuna with arugula, wild mushrooms and truffle aïoli

4 x medium (5 oz.) tuna fillets ●

2 tablespoons olive oil

4½ cups (1 lb.) wild ●
mushrooms, well trimmed and
cut into even-sized pieces

⅓ cup (¾ stick) ●
unsalted butter

8 cups (1 lb.) arugula leaves ●

3 tablespoons aïoli ●
(home-made is best)

Few drops of truffle oil ●

Heat a heavy skillet until very hot. Season the tuna fillets. Add one tablespoon of the olive oil to the skillet and add the tuna fillets. Sear for a minute or two, depending on the thickness of the fillets, until well seared but still pink in the middle.

Meanwhile, heat a separate skillet and a saucepan. Add the remaining tablespoon of olive oil to the skillet and then add the wild mushrooms. Sauté for a minute, then add 4 tablespoons of the butter and season to taste. Sauté for another few minutes until tender.

Add the remaining butter to the saucepan, swirl around and then quickly tip in the arugula. Stir-fry until just wilted, then remove from the heat and season. Mix the aïoli with enough truffle oil to taste. Arrange the wilted arugula in the middle of warmed wide-rimmed bowls and place tuna on top. Spoon the wild mushrooms around the edges of the bowls and finally add tiny dots of the truffle aïoli to serve.

grilled tilapia with shallots, tomatoes and fennel

1 tablespoon olive oil

1 fennel bulb, well trimmed and ●
shredded

¼ teaspoon fresh thyme leaves ●

4 x medium (5–6 oz.) tilapia ●
fillets, unskinned

4 ripe plum tomatoes, sliced ●

4 shallots, sliced ●

2 garlic cloves, finely chopped ●

Preheat the oven to 350°F and preheat the broiler. Lightly oil a round baking dish and layer up the fennel, sprinkling the thyme and a little seasoning as you go. Score the skin of each tilapia fillet three times, season and arrange on top of the fennel, skin-side up.

Arrange the tomato slices in a layer on top, again seasoning as you go and then scatter over the shallots and garlic. Drizzle over the olive oil and cover loosely with aluminium foil. Bake for 8 minutes, then remove the aluminium foil and cook under the broiler for another 5 minutes or so, basting occasionally or until the fennel is cooked through and tender. Serve immediately with a bowl of boiled new potatoes, if liked.

Monkfish is a firm-fleshed fish, which can withstand cooking methods that are normally more suited to meat. It also benefits from resting which allows all the juices to settle down before serving. I like to serve this with a side order of sautéed spinach or just some seasonal vegetables.

fried monkfish

with preserved shallot sauce

SERVES 2

2 x smallish (7 oz.) potatoes ●

½ cup (1 stick) ●
unsalted butter

2 x medium (6 oz.) ●
monkfish fillets

4 shallots, skins intact ●

⅔ cup (¼ pint) fish or ●
vegetable broth

½ lemon, pips removed ●

Preheat the oven to 350°F. Peel the potatoes and using a sharp knife, shave into very fine slices. Wash in a sieve and press dry with a clean dish towel. Season and tip into a bowl. Melt 2 tablespoons of the butter in a small skillet and pour over the potatoes, tossing to combine. Arrange the potatoes in an overlapping layer in a large ovenproof dish and bake for 25–30 minutes or until completely tender and golden brown.

Meanwhile, heat a large heavy skillet or roasting pan. Season the monkfish fillets. Add a knob of butter to the skillet and then quickly fry the monkfish until well seared all over. Tip in the shallots, shaking the skillet until they are well coated in the juices, then transfer to the oven and bake for 10 minutes or until the fish is just tender. Remove from the oven, then transfer the fish to a warmed plate and keep warm.

Place the skillet or roasting pan back on the stove and pour in the broth, then allow to de-glaze, scraping the bottom of the pan or skillet to remove any sediment. Return to the oven for another 5–10 minutes or until the shallots are soft when pierced with a knife. Carefully peel the shallots and place in a small saucepan with the cooking liquid and whisk in the remaining butter. Season to taste and add a squeeze of lemon juice. Pass through a sieve into a clean saucepan and keep warm.

Arrange the potato slices on hot serving plates in the shape of a crown and place a monkfish fillet in the center of each one. Pour over the sauce and serve at once.

You can use John Dory or turbot equally well in this dish. As usual, get your fishmonger to do all the dirty work and give you the fillets.

fillet of turbot with cucumber spaghetti and herb crème fraîche

SERVES 4

1 cup (7 fl.oz.) crème fraîche or sour cream

Juice of ½ lemon

1 tablespoon chopped mixed herbs (such as dill, chervil and chives)

2 cucumbers

2 large carrots

2 tablespoons olive oil

4 x medium (5 oz.) turbot fillets, unskinned

Place the crème fraîche or sour cream in a bowl and add the lemon juice (reserving half a teaspoon) and the herbs. Season to taste and mix well, then cover with plastic wrap and place in the fridge to firm up or overnight is fine.

Peel each cucumber, then cut in half and remove the pips with a teaspoon; discard. Slice the cucumbers into long thin strips so that it resembles "spaghetti" and place in a bowl. Peel the carrots and slice just like the cucumbers. Add to the cucumbers and gently mix to combine the colors. Add the reserved half a teaspoon of lemon juice, one teaspoon of the oil and season generously, mixing gently to combine. Cover with plastic wrap and set aside to allow the flavors to mingle.

Heat a non-stick skillet until very hot. Add the remaining olive oil to the skillet and then add the turbot fillets, skin-side down. Cook for 4–5 minutes, until the skin is crisp and golden, then turn over and cook for another minute until tender. Season to taste.

Arrange the cucumber spaghetti in wide-rimmed bowls and place a piece of turbot on top of each one. Quickly dip two tablespoons into boiling water and use to shape the herb crème fraîche or sour cream into a quenelle (oval ball) – you will probably have some left-over that can be used for another dish. Place one on each piece of turbot and serve immediately with cumin-roasted new potatoes, if liked.

take 6
ingredients | fish and shellfish

I always loved the combination of cabbage with the spicy aromatic flavors of cumin. Add the crusted salmon and you've got a superb dinner party dish, most of which can be prepared well in advance. The cous cous crust really works well with salmon, but wouldn't necessarily suit all fish – perhaps this is because salmon is naturally quite a fatty fish.

cous cous-crusted salmon with spiced cabbage and cumin sour cream

SERVES 4

2 teaspoons cumin seeds ●

1/2 cup (31/2 fl.oz.) sour cream ●

1 dark green Savoy cabbage ●

2/3 cup (31/2 oz.) cous cous ●

4 x medium (5 oz.) salmon ●
fillets, skinned

3 tablespoons olive oil

4 tablespoons heavy cream ●

Heat a small skillet. Add half of the cumin seeds and toast for a few minutes until aromatic. Leave to cool a little, then stir into the sour cream and chill for at least 2 hours to firm up or overnight is fine.

Remove the leaves from the cabbage and cut out the thick stalks, then blanch the leaves in a large saucepan of boiling water for 3 minutes. Drain, and immediately refresh in cold water. Pat dry with paper towels and finely shred. Place in a bowl and cover with plastic wrap, then chill until ready to use.

Heat a large heavy skillet. Place the cous cous on a plate and dip in the salmon fillets until completely coated. Add the olive oil to the frying pan and then add the salmon fillets, presentation-side down and cook for 8–10 minutes, turning once until the salmon is just tender and the cous cous is lightly golden.

Meanwhile, heat a sauté skillet. Pour in the cream and add the remaining cumin seeds. Bring to a simmer, then tip in the blanched shredded cabbage and sauté for few minutes until the cream has slightly reduced but the cabbage is still holding its color.

Drain the salmon fillets on paper towels. Spoon the spiced cabbage into warmed wide-rimmed bowls and arrange a piece of salmon on top of each one. Quickly dip two tablespoons into boiling water and use to shape the cumin sour cream into quenelles (oval balls.) Place a quenelle on top of each piece of salmon and serve immediately with sauté potatoes, if liked.

take 6
ingredients | fish and
shellfish

Thick cod fillets are excellent for good fish and French fries, especially with a crispy lager beer batter (helped by the addition of the melted brown butter). For me, duck or goose fat make the best possible French fries, and the latter is now readily available in cans from most major supermarkets. However, vegetable oil is a perfectly good alternative and works out much cheaper!

nora's fish and chips

SERVES 4

Vegetable oil, for deep-frying

2¹/₄ lbs. (about 7 medium) ● *potatoes, peeled*

1 tablespoon (¹/₂ oz.) ● *unsalted butter*

4 x small–medium (4 oz.) thick ● *cod fillets, skinned*

1 cup (4 oz.) self-rising flour, ● *plus extra for dusting*

1 egg, lightly beaten ●

About 5 tablespoons (3 fl.oz.) ● *lager beer*

Heat the vegetable oil to 350°F in an electric deep-fat fryer or large skillet (use a cooking thermometer if necessary) and preheat the oven to its lowest setting.

While the oil is heating, prepare the potatoes. First cut a slice, ¹/₂-inch thick, off the potato lengthwise, then, using the flat side as a base, cut the potato into 2-inch slices. Finally cut each slice into 2-inch square pieces. Place them in a bowl of cold water until ready to cook.

Drain the potatoes and dry well in a clean dish towel. Carefully add the potatoes to the hot fat and fry them for 12–15 minutes until crisp and golden brown.

Lift the basket clear of the oil and shake off any excess. Tip the French fries into a bowl lined with plenty of paper towels and place in the oven to keep warm while you finish cooking the fish, but don't close the door or the French fries will go soggy.

Place the butter in a small skillet and melt until it turns a nut-brown color but is not burnt, then immediately remove from the heat. Season the cod fillets and dip them in the flour to coat each piece, shaking off any excess. Gradually whisk the remaining flour in a bowl with the egg and enough lager beer to make a thick batter.

Stir the brown butter into the flour mixture and add a good pinch of salt, then dip in the dusted cod fillets and fry in the deep-fat fryer for about 5 minutes until golden brown, then drain on a large plate lined with paper towels to remove any excess oil.

Remove the French fries from the oven as soon as the fish is cooked, sprinkle with salt and arrange on warmed serving plates with the crispy battered cod. Serve at once with lemon wedges, some minted peas and tartare sauce, if liked.

When we think of cod the first thing that springs to mind is good old fish and French fries. Although not one to criticize an institution, this is a much healthier alternative. Once you've tried it you may well admit that lentils are well "on par" with French fries.

cod on smoked lentils

with chorizo oil

SERVES 4

4 tablespoons olive oil

1 onion, finely chopped ●

1 tablespoon fresh thyme leaves ●

1½ cups (11 oz.) Puy lentils ●

4 oz. piece of smoked thick-sliced bacon, chopped ●

4 x medium (5 oz.) cod fillets, unskinned ●

1 raw chorizo sausage, cut into slices (about 7 oz. in total) ●

Heat a deep-sided saucepan. Add two tablespoons of the oil and then add the onion and thyme leaves. Sweat for 3–4 minutes until softened but not colored, then tip in the lentils, stirring for 30 seconds until they are well coated. Pour in enough water to cover the lentils by 3 inches. Add the bacon and simmer the lentils for 40–45 minutes, or according to packet instructions, until the lentils are tender but still firm, then strain.

Heat a non-stick skillet. Season the cod and make a few shallow slashes in the skin. Add the remaining two tablespoons of oil to the skillet and then add the cod fillets, skin-side down. Cook for 3–4 minutes until the skin is crispy and lightly golden, then turn over and cook for another 2–3 minutes until the cod is just tender and firm to the touch. Transfer the cod to a baking dish and keep warm.

Add the chorizo to the skillet and cook over a low heat for a minute or so on each side until the chorizo is sizzling and cooked through. Meanwhile, spoon the lentils into warmed wide-rimmed bowls and place a piece of cod on top of each one, skin-side up. Arrange the chorizo slices around the edge of each bowl and drizzle the pan juices on top. Garnish with small mounds of dressed arugula leaves, if liked and serve immediately.

take 6
ingredients | fish and
shellfish

Salmon is an extremely versatile fish and lends itself to all manner of dishes. This dish literally takes minutes to prepare and will serve a good number of people with perfectly cooked fish. It is very important to use a very hot broiler for this recipe with an even heat. The idea is that the salmon has just started to cook, but no more. For an extra kick, add half a finely chopped red chile to the salsa.

gratinated salmon

with vegetable salsa

SERVES 4–6

4 heaped tablespoons chopped fresh cilantro ●

1 red onion, finely chopped ●

4 plum tomatoes, peeled, pitted and diced ●

Juice of 1 lemon ●

½ cup (4 oz.) mayonnaise (preferably home-made) ●

1¼ lbs. fresh salmon fillet, skinned and thinly sliced ●

A little olive oil

To make the salsa; place half the cilantro in a bowl with the red onion, plum tomatoes and lemon juice, and season to taste. Mix to combine, then set aside for 30 minutes to allow the flavors to combine.

Preheat the broiler. Mix the remaining cilantro in a bowl with the mayonnaise and season to taste. Arrange the salmon slices on a large lightly oiled baking sheet so that they are overlapping.

Spread the cilantro mayonnaise on top of the salmon and broil for 30 seconds to 1 minute until the mayonnaise is bubbling and lightly golden and the salmon has just warmed through.

Carefully flake the fillets, combine with the salsa and arrange on warmed serving plates. Serve at once with a mixed salad and some bread, if liked.

take 6
ingredients | fish and
shellfish

I like to serve this as a light main course, but it also makes a perfect appetizer. The flavors may sound unusual but combined, you get the most fantastic taste explosion with every mouthful. For an extra dimension sprinkle very fine Granny Smith apple brunoise (dice) around the edge of the plate just before serving. The vanilla-infused olive oil can be made well in advance and will keep happily for up to two weeks in a sterilized bottle.

vanilla potatoes
with tiger shrimp and lemon syrup

SERVES 4

2 vanilla pods ●

1/3 cup (3 1/2 fl.oz.) olive oil, plus
1 tablespoon

1 lemon (preferably unwaxed) ●

4 teaspoons superfine sugar ●

4 small potatoes, peeled and ●
each one cut into 7 slices,
1/2-inch thick (ends discarded)

20 large raw tiger shrimp, ●
peeled and cleaned

28 sprigs lambs lettuce ●

Cut the vanilla pods in half and using a teaspoon, scrape out the pips. Place in a bowl with 1/3 cup (3 1/2 fl.oz.) of the olive oil, stirring to combine. Cover with plastic wrap and set aside for 48 hours to allow the flavors to infuse.

Pare the rind from the lemon and then cut into fine julienne strips. Cut the lemon in half and squeeze out the juice; set aside. Place the strips in a saucepan and just cover with water. Bring to a boil, then remove the julienne with a slotted spoon and refresh under cold running water.

Return the julienne to the saucepan that still has the water in it and stir in the sugar and lemon juice, then bring to a simmer and cook gently for 5–10 minutes until you have achieved a syrup-like consistency. Allow to cool completely.

Place the potatoes in a small saucepan and pour over the infused olive oil, then cook over a very low heat until *al dente*. Remove from the heat and leave to cool in the oil.

Heat a non-stick skillet. Add the remaining tablespoon of oil to the pan and then add the shrimp. Cook for 20 seconds on each side until just tender. Season to taste.

To serve, drain the potatoes from the oil, reserving the oil. Arrange the lambs lettuce and drained potato slices alternately in a circle on serving plates – you'll need about seven slices of potato per portion. Place the tiger shrimp in the center and drizzle over the lemon syrup and garnish with drops of the reserved vanilla olive oil. Serve at once.

take 6
ingredients | fish and
shellfish

Buy a good piece of turbot from your fishmonger for this recipe and ask him to fillet and skin it into the required portions. However, this dish would also work very well with sea bass or thick cod fillets – the choice is yours.

grilled turbot with avocado puree
and grilled pancetta

SERVES 4

2 large ripe avocados ●

2 lemons, halved and ●
pips removed

2 red chiles, seeded ●
and chopped

2 shallots, chopped ●

8 thinly sliced pieces (4 oz.) ●
pancetta (Italian thick-sliced
bacon)

4 x turbot fillets, skinned ●

2 tablespoons olive oil

Peel the avocados and remove the pits, then squeeze over some of the lemon juice to prevent them from going black. Place in a food processor or liquidizer with the chiles and shallots, then whizz to a puree. Transfer to a non-metallic bowl, cover immediately with plastic wrap and chill until needed.

Preheat the broiler. Arrange the pancetta on a broiler rack and cook until crisp and lightly golden. Drain on a large plate lined with paper towels.

Heat a large non-stick skillet. Season the turbot fillets. Add the olive oil and then add the turbot, presentation-side down and cook for 2–3 minutes until golden – you may have to do this in batches, depending on the size of your skillet and keep them warm in a low oven while you finish cooking the remainder. Turn the fillets over and cook for another 2 minutes until just tender and lightly golden.

Set a 2³/₄-inch cooking ring mold on each serving plate and fill with the avocado puree, smoothing over the top with a palette knife. Carefully lay a fish fillet on top of each one and arrange the crispy pancetta criss-crossed over the fish. Serve at once.

meat

Veal at its best is tender, succulent to the point of stickiness and truly delicious. The best milk-fed veal is very pale in color and normally very expensive but perfect for this type of dish as the cutlets should be just briefly fried. Look out for the quality-assured label to ensure that it has been sympathetically reared.

veal cutlet with roasted asparagus,
warm lemon and tarragon vinaigrette

SERVES 4

1 lemon (preferably unwaxed) ●

16 small new potatoes, ●
well scrubbed

²/₃ cup (¹/₄ pint) olive oil,
plus 2 tablespoons

4 veal cutlets ●

2 fresh tarragon sprigs, ●
2 tablespoons chopped fresh
tarragon

³/₄ cup (7 fl.oz.) chicken broth ●

20 asparagus spears, ●
well trimmed

Pare the rind from the lemon and plunge into boiling water. Blanch for 10 seconds, then remove and refresh under cold running water before repeating. Juice the lemon.

Place the potatoes in a saucepan of boiling salted water, bring to a boil, then cover and simmer for 10–12 minutes or until completely tender.

Heat a large heavy skillet. Add two tablespoons of olive oil, then add the veal cutlets and the blanched lemon rind. Season the cutlets and cook for 3–4 minutes on each side until just tender.

Add the whole tarragon sprigs to the skillet for the final couple of minutes of the cooking time. Remove the cutlets from the skillet on to a warmed plate and leave to rest.

Pour the broth into the saucepan and de-glaze, scraping the bottom of the pan with a wooden spoon to remove any sediment. Cook for a couple of minutes until slightly reduced.

Meanwhile, cook the asparagus in a saucepan of boiling salted water for about 3 minutes until just tender.

Pass the sauce through a fine sieve into a clean saucepan and then stir in the remaining ²/₃ cup (¹/₄ pint) of olive oil, the lemon juice and chopped fresh tarragon. Whisk over a low heat until just warmed through.

Drain the potatoes and the asparagus, refreshing the asparagus under cold running water and arrange on warmed plates with the rested veal cutlets. Spoon over the tarragon vinaigrette and serve at once.

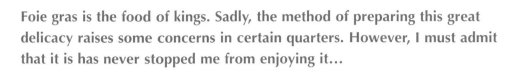

Foie gras is the food of kings. Sadly, the method of preparing this great delicacy raises some concerns in certain quarters. However, I must admit that it is has never stopped me from enjoying it...

pan-fried beef fillet with fried quail egg and foie gras butter with truffle

SERVES 4

- 12 oz. foie gras (goose or duck liver)

- ¼ cup (½ stick) unsalted butter, at room temperature

- 2 tablespoons (1 oz.) black truffle shavings

4 tablespoons olive oil

- 4 x medium (6 oz.) beef fillet steaks

- 8 quail eggs

Trim the foie gras – you'll need about 1 oz. to flavor the butter, then cut the rest into four even-sized slices. Place the foie gras trimmings in a bowl with the butter and half of the truffle shavings. Mix until well combined, then make into a cylinder shape that is about 2 inches long before rolling in the remaining truffle shavings. Place on a small plate, cover loosely with plastic wrap and chill until ready to use.

Heat a heavy skillet until hot. Add two tablespoons of the olive oil and then add the steaks. Cook gently for a couple of minutes on each side (a bit longer if you don't like your meat so rare). Remove from the heat and leave to rest in a warm place for a few minutes.

Heat a separate large skillet. Add the remaining two tablespoons of olive oil and carefully break in the quail eggs. Cook for 30 seconds or so, basting with the olive oil as you go. Season to taste.

Heat a heavy skillet until very hot. Season the slices of foie gras. Add to the pan and sear for 30 seconds to 1 minute on each side until just tender and caramelized.

Remove the butter from the fridge and cut it into four even-sized discs. Place a steak in the middle of each warmed wide-rimmed bowl and place a disc of the foie gras butter on top. Garnish with the fried quail eggs and serve immediately with French fries and fresh beans, if liked.

take 6
ingredients | meat

For me, this is the ultimate comfort food. The secret to getting these corned beef hash croquettes really crispy is to move them about in the skillet as little as possible until a decent crust forms. It also helps to have the croquettes well chilled before cooking them in a good-quality non-stick skillet.

corned beef hash with poached eggs

SERVES 4

8 medium (2½ lbs.) floury potatoes, well scrubbed ●

5 tablespoons (3 fl.oz.) heavy cream ●

4½ cups (1 lb.) cooked corned beef, diced ●

4 eggs, plus 3 egg yolks ●

2 tablespoons (1 oz.) snipped fresh chives, plus whole chives to garnish ●

A little all-purpose flour, for dusting ●

About 2 tablespoons olive oil

take 6
ingredients | meat

Cook the potatoes in a covered saucepan of boiling salted water for 20–30 minutes, depending on their size until completely tender. Drain and allow to steam in a colander. Once they are cool enough to handle, peel away the skins and then mash until completely smooth – you'll need about 1lb. in total.

Place the cream in a small saucepan and bring to a boil, then allow it to reduce slightly, stirring occasionally. Place the mashed potatoes in a bowl with the corned beef and mix in the egg yolks to combine. Beat in the reduced cream mixture and chives, then season generously. Allow the mixture to cool and firm up slightly.

Using lightly floured hands, shape the potato mixture into a roll that is about 3 inches in diameter. Cut into 3-inch sections, shape into croquettes (cylinder shapes) and arrange on a flat baking sheet – you'll need twelve in total. Cover loosely with plastic wrap and chill for at least 2 hours or overnight to allow the mixture to rest and firm up.

Heat a large pan with 9 cups (4 pints) of water. Break each whole egg into the water where it is bubbling, then move the pan to the edge of the heat and simmer gently for 2–3 minutes. Remove with a slotted spoon, then plunge into a bowl of iced water. When cold, trim down any ragged ends from the cooked egg white. These will keep perfectly well in a bowl covered with cold water in the fridge for a couple of days.

Heat a large non-stick skillet. Lightly dust each croquette again in a little flour, brushing off any excess. Add the olive oil to the skillet and fry the hash croquettes for 10–15 minutes until crisp and golden brown, turning occasionally. Add the poached eggs to a saucepan of boiling salted water and cook for a minute or so just to warm through. Arrange the corned beef hash croquettes in warmed wide-rimmed bowls and place a poached egg on top of each one. Garnish with the whole chives and serve at once.

This is my version of a French man's posh stew but it's worth bearing in mind that the finished result will only be as good as the original raw ingredients. Pickled goat cheeses are my new favorite ingredient and can be purchased in most good cheese shops, but if you want to make your own check out the introduction on page 57 (Beet Risotto with Pickled Goat Cheese and Charred Chicken Livers) which shows just how easy they are to prepare.

lamb fillets with olives,
thyme, red onions, and goat cheese

SERVES 4

4 x small (4 oz.) lamb fillets ● (best end)

5 tablespoons (3 fl.oz.) extra virgin olive oil

4 red onions, sliced ●

1/2 cup (4 fl.oz.) white wine ●

1 tablespoon (1/2 oz.) chopped ● fresh lemon thyme

1/4 cup (1 oz.) black olives ●

2 oz. small goat cheese balls, ● pickled (see above)

Trim all the fat from the lamb fillets and cut it into 1-inch dice. Heat a large heavy saucepan. Season the lamb. Add two tablespoons of the olive oil to the saucepan, and then tip in the lamb. Sauté until well browned all over, then tip in the red onions and continue to sauté for another couple of minutes until the onions have softened.

Pour the wine into the pan and allow to de-glaze, scraping the bottom of the saucepan with a wooden spoon to remove any sediment. Stir in the lemon thyme leaves, season to taste, and then stir in the remaining olive oil. Simmer gently for 10–15 minutes or until the sauce has reduced and thickened slightly.

Preheat the broiler. Stir the olives and goat cheese into the pan and cook for another minute or so just to warm through. Divide among warmed, heatproof wide-rimmed bowls and place each one under the broiler for 2–3 minutes to "gratinate" the top. Serve at once with a green salad, if liked.

Having grown up in Ireland, Sunday lunch with Granny didn't necessarily mean Sunday roast. This is one of the recipes that made us return again and again to the late Nora Gallagher's hearth. Ask your butcher to cut you the pieces of lamb chump – in case there is any confusion they come from the top end of the leg of lamb.

roast chump of lamb with garlic

SERVES 4

1¼ lbs. (about 12) new potatoes, scrubbed ●

4 tablespoons olive oil

6 garlic cloves, finely chopped ●

2 teaspoons fresh thyme leaves ●

4 x medium (6 oz.) lamb ● chumps

2 zucchini, cut into ● rough triangles

4 ripe, firm tomatoes, quartered ●

Preheat the oven to 350°F. Cut the potatoes into ½-inch slices and place in a large roasting pan with two tablespoons of the olive oil and season generously. Toss to coat and roast for 20 minutes, then add the garlic and thyme, tossing again to coat and roast for another 8–10 minutes or until the potatoes are crisp and tender. Leave the garlic and thyme juices in the roasting tin.

Meanwhile, heat a heavy roasting pan on the hob. Season the lamb chumps. Add the remaining two tablespoons of olive oil to the pan and then add the lamb chumps. Sear on each side for a minute or so until well sealed and golden brown in patches. Place each chump, skin-side down and roast for 10–12 minutes until just tender but still slightly pink in the middle. Transfer to a warmed dish and leave to rest in a warm place.

Add the zucchini to the same roasting pan with the remaining garlic and thyme, tossing to coat in the juices and roast for 5 minutes. Add the tomatoes, tossing again to coat and cook for another 5 minutes, remembering to turn the vegetables occasionally.

Meanwhile, arrange the potatoes on warmed serving plates and spoon over the cooked vegetables. Carve the lamb and arrange on top, then drizzle all of the meat and vegetable juices on top as a sauce. Serve immediately.

take 6
ingredients | meat

96

This is actually made in a very similar way to sushi except that you are using steak instead of seaweed to make a roll. The combination of flavors is truly sensational, especially served with a teriyaki dipping sauce and some Thai sticky rice. The sirloin steak needs to be a thin slice in one whole piece, otherwise you'll have great difficulty making the recipe work. Alternatively, try securing the roll with cocktail sticks which can be removed before carving.

seared beef roll
with ginger, carrot and peppers

SERVES 4

1 lb. thinly sliced piece of sirloin steak, trimmed

4-inch piece (4 oz.) fresh ginger root, peeled and cut into julienne

2 large carrots, peeled and cut into julienne

6 jalapeño chiles, pitted and cut into julienne

2 red or yellow bell peppers, halved, seeded and cut into julienne

1 bottle/can of hearts of palm, drained and cut into julienne

A little olive oil

take 6
ingredients | meat

Place the sirloin steak on a piece of plastic wrap and cover with another piece. Flatten with a rolling pin until you have achieved a rectangle that is 3-inch x 4-inch in total, trimming down any ragged pieces around the edges – these can be used in another dish or for a sauce. Remove and discard the plastic wrap.

Layer the ginger, carrots, jalapeño chiles, bell peppers and hearts of palm julienne on to the middle of the beef, leaving two-thirds of the meat uncovered with at least a 1/2-inch border at the bottom edge. Roll up the beef around the vegetables, forming a tight tube similar to a sushi roll.

Heat a large frying skillet. Add a little olive oil and when the oil is smoking, add the sirloin roll to the skillet and sear evenly on all sides. Using a pair of tongs, remove the beef roll from the skillet and transfer to a chopping board. Cut in half and then into quarters. Arrange in warmed wide-rimmed bowls and serve with a small dish of teriyaki dipping sauce and some Thai sticky rice, if liked.

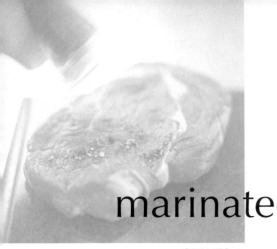

This is a quick, easy and healthy dish which I often prepare at home. It has loads of flavor for minimum effort. The fresh zingy flavor of root ginger comes through and the sauce created is similar to teriyaki, but not quite as sweet. I like to serve this with fragrant jasmine rice and a green salad.

marinated sirloin skewers

SERVES 4

1 onion, thinly sliced ●

2-inch piece (2 oz.) fresh ●
ginger root, peeled and cut
into julienne

¹/₂ cup (4 fl.oz.) dark soy sauce ●

1 lb. sirloin steak, cut into ●
1-inch cubes

4 tablespoons olive oil

1¹/₃ cups (4 oz.) shiitake ●
mushrooms, sliced

2 carrots, peeled and shredded ●

Place the onion, ginger and soy sauce in a shallow non-metallic dish. Add the steak cubes, stirring to combine, then cover with plastic wrap and chill for at least 3 hours or overnight is fine.

Heat a large non-stick skillet until hot. Drain the beef from the marinade, reserving it to use later, then thread the beef on to 6-inch wooden skewers. Add the oil to the skillet and when the oil begins to smoke, sear the skewers on all sides – you may have to do this in two batches, depending on the size of your skillet. Transfer to a warmed plate and keep warm.

Add the mushrooms and carrots to the same skillet that you have cooked the beef in, then sauté for 2 minutes. Add four tablespoons of the reserved marinade, reduce the heat and continue to cook for about 1 minute, stirring occasionally. Arrange the skewers on warmed serving plates with the vegetables and spoon over any remaining sauce. Serve at once.

take 6
ingredients | meat

I like to temper my Thai curries with a dash of Thai fish sauce and lime juice just before serving. Traditionally, this curry would be garnished with fresh cilantro leaves and shredded scallions and served with Thai sticky rice. But these, of course, are all optional extras.

thai red pork and pumpkin curry

SERVES 4

2 tablespoons olive oil

1 lb. lean pork, cut into 1-inch cubes ●

2 red chiles, pitted and finely chopped ●

2 tablespoons Thai red curry paste ●

2 x 6 oz. cartons coconut cream ●

1³/₄ cups (³/₄ pint) chicken broth ●

1 lb. pumpkin, cut into 1-inch cubes ●

Heat a large saucepan. Add the olive oil and then tip in the pork and sear over a fairly high heat until lightly browned. Add the chiles and red curry paste and cook for 3–5 minutes, stirring with a wooden spatula.

Pour the coconut cream into the saucepan and mix to combine, scraping the bottom of the saucepan to remove any sediment. Add the chicken broth and pumpkin, then bring to a boil and reduce the heat. Simmer for 25–30 minutes or until the pumpkin is completely tender but still holding its shape and the sauce has slightly reduced. Season to taste and ladle into warmed wide-rimmed bowls to serve.

take 6
ingredients | meat

poultry and game

Partridge is one of my favorite game birds. It is in season from early autumn until early spring, but you may still find it for sale up to 10 days after the end of the season. It has a paler flesh than most other game birds. The young birds are at their best at the beginning of autumn and are simply divine roasted and served as described below. This recipe only serves the breasts but the remaining carcass will make the most fantastic stock.

roasted partridge
with thyme and truffle mash

SERVES 4

3 medium (1 lb.) floury potatoes

1–2 tablespoons olive oil

4 plump oven-ready partridges

Handful fresh thyme sprigs

1/3 cup (3/4 stick) unsalted butter

1 cup (9 fl.oz.) heavy cream

2 tablespoons (1 oz.) black truffle, finely chopped

Preheat the oven to 475°F. Place the potatoes in a saucepan of boiling salted water, cover and simmer for 20–25 minutes, depending on the size of the potatoes until completely tender.

Heat a large ovenproof skillet. Season the partridges. Add a thin film of olive oil to the skillet and then add the partridges and thyme sprigs. Cook the partridges on all sides until golden brown, basting constantly – this should take no more than 10 minutes. Transfer to the oven and roast for another 3–5 minutes, basting occasionally or until the partridges are just cooked through. Remove from the oven and leave to rest for about 5 minutes in a warm place, before carefully carving off the breasts.

Meanwhile, drain the potatoes and return to the saucepan to dry out, shaking it occasionally. Remove from the heat and leave until cool enough to handle, then peel and either pass through a mouli or potato ricer. Return to the pan and beat in the butter, cream and truffle. Season to taste.

Divide the mash among warmed wide-rimmed bowls and arrange two partridge breasts on top of each one. Serve immediately with a spoonful of cranberry or Cumberland sauce on the side, if liked.

I just love to make this dish with mallard, wild ducks which are in season from early autumn to the beginning of spring. However, I usually wait until about mid autumn before ordering any, when the birds have a bit more weight on them. Expect to find the breasts smaller than farmed duck, but leaner and much tastier.

crispy duck breast

with rosemary polenta

SERVES 4

● 1¹/₃ cups (7 oz.) polenta

● 2 tablespoons chopped
fresh rosemary

● 2³/₄ cups (7 oz.) freshly
shredded Parmesan

● ¹/₄ cup (¹/₂ stick) unsalted butter

● 4 x medium (6 oz.) duck
breasts, well trimmed

● ³/₄–1 cup (6 oz.) mascarpone
cheese

Bring 2¹/₂ cups (1 pint) of water to a boil in a large deep-sided saucepan, season it, then pour in the polenta in a thin, steady stream, stirring vigorously with a wooden spoon in your other hand. Reduce the heat to medium, stir in the rosemary and cook, stirring continuously until the mixture comes to a boil.

Now reduce the heat again to low, and simmer for 5–45 minutes depending on packet instructions, stirring constantly. Be very careful when you stir, as polenta tends to imitate volcanic mud and can give you a nasty burn. When the polenta is cooked, remove from the heat and stir in the Parmesan and butter. Season to taste and keep warm – it won't keep "wet" like this for too long so don't make it too far in advance.

Meanwhile, heat a non-stick skillet. Season the duck breasts, then add to the skillet, skin-side down. Cook for 6–8 minutes until the skin is crisp and golden brown. Turn over and cook for another 2–4 minutes or until the duck is tender but still pink in the middle. Remove the skillet from the heat and leave to rest in a warm place for 10 minutes.

Carve each duck breast diagonally into slices. Divide the polenta between warmed wide-rimmed bowls and arrange the duck on top. Quickly dip two tablespoons in boiling water and use to make the mascarpone cheese into quenelles (oval balls). Place one on the side of each duck breast and serve immediately with fine green beans, if liked.

For a rich, tasty and succulent meal, look no further – the depth of flavor in this dish is fantastic, especially when you consider that it only has six ingredients in the recipe. Goose is still very much a seasonal bird and they normally don't tend to appear on our shelves before autumn. A whole goose at this time of year weighs approximately 10 lbs. which is a good size for this recipe.

roasted goose breast
with pineapple, chile and buttermilk

SERVES 4

4 goose breast fillets ●

4 tablespoons wild honey ●

1 small baby pineapple ●

2 red chiles, pitted and ● finely chopped

1 tablespoon chopped ● fresh sage

2¹/₂ cups (1 pint) buttermilk ●

Preheat the oven to 450°F. Heat a large skillet. Add the goose breasts, skin-side down and allow the fat to render down, draining any excess into a bowl. Continue this process for 3–5 minutes until the skin is golden brown.

Remove the goose breasts from the skillet and transfer to a wire rack that is set in a roasting pan. Brush each breast with the honey, then roast for 5–7 minutes or until medium rare. Leave to rest in a warm place for about 10 minutes, then pour away all the excess fat from the roasting pan.

To prepare the pineapple, cut off the leaf crown and bottom so that it sits flat. Using a sharp knife, remove the skin by cutting down the length of the fruit, then cut the flesh into wedges lengthways, remove the core and cut into thin slices.

Arrange the pineapple slices in a layer in the roasting pan with the sediment from the fat. Place the goose breasts on top and sprinkle over the chiles and sage. Pour around the buttermilk, cover the pan with aluminium foil, making a small incision in the top to allow the steam to escape and bake for another 3–5 minutes or until the goose breasts are completely tender. Make sure you have removed all the goose fat from the tin, otherwise the buttermilk may split. Remove the aluminium foil and bring the dish straight to the table. Serve on warmed serving plates with plenty of creamed potatoes, if liked.

take 6
ingredients | poultry and game

Quails might seem rather extravagant and somewhat daunting, but they are incredibly easy to cook, not that expensive and readily available. They taste like very delicate chicken – just be careful not to over-cook them as they tend to dry out. If you get a chance to get some, go for it. Boneless quail are available in most major supermarkets or you could always try and get your butcher to prepare them for you – just give some advance notice.

whole boneless quail with peaches, swiss chard and muscat wine

SERVES 4

- *4 whole boneless oven-ready quail*
- *2 level tablespoons (1 oz.) light brown sugar*
- *8 ripe peaches, halved and pitted*
- *2¹/₂ cups (1 pint) muscat wine*
- *2 vanilla pods, split*
- *2 head of Swiss chard, cut into julienne*

Preheat the oven to 400°F. Place the quails in the center of a large ovenproof dish, using cocktail sticks to help keep the shape of each bird. Roast in the oven for 3–5 minutes or until golden brown, then drizzle with the olive oil and season to taste. Return to the oven and cook for another minute or two or until the juices just begin to run.

Remove from the oven and sprinkle the sugar over the quails. Surround with the peaches and pour in the muscat wine. Tuck in the vanilla pods and sprinkle the Swiss chard julienne on top. Return to oven and cook for another 5–7 minutes or until the quails are completely tender. Bring the dish straight to the table and serve in warmed wide-rimmed bowls.

Poussins are the smallest chickens available to buy. I like them because they are tender and very quick to cook. If you are worried about preparing the poussin, just ask the butcher to do it for you – it's their job! Here I'm serving them with a parsnip puree and some slices of spicy chorizo sausage. I've simmered the parsnips in milk instead of water for a richer flavor before mashing them to a puree with cream.

roasted poussin with parsnip puree

SERVES 4

8 medium to large (12 oz.) ●
parsnips, roughly chopped

2 1/2 cups (1 pint) milk ●

4 tablespoons olive oil

2 raw chorizo sausages ●

4 oven-ready poussins ●

1/3 cup (3 1/2 fl.oz.) heavy cream ●

Preheat the oven to 350°F. Place the parsnips in a saucepan with the milk and simmer for 15–20 minutes until completely tender and softened. Heat a skillet. Add two tablespoons of the olive oil and cook the chorizo sausages for 5–10 minutes, depending on their size until cooked through and tender, turning occasionally. Drain on paper towels, reserving the cooking oil.

Cut through the skin of one of the poussins where the thigh joins the body, then cut right down between the ball and socket joint to remove the leg completely. Repeat with the other leg and remaining poussins. Carefully cut the breasts off each poussin. Season each poussin portion and discard the carcasses or use them for broth.

Place the remaining olive oil in a heavy-based roasting pan. Add the poussin legs and cook for a few minutes until lightly golden, then add the breasts and continue to cook for another few minutes, basting constantly until well sealed and lightly golden all over. Transfer the roasting pan to the oven and cook for another 3–5 minutes or until the legs and breasts are tender and cooked through. Remove from the oven and leave to rest in a warm place for 5–10 minutes.

Drain the parsnips and return to the saucepan for a couple of minutes to dry out, then mash to a puree. Beat in the cream and season to taste. Using a sharp knife, cut the cooked chorizo into slices. Divide the parsnip puree between warmed wide-rimmed bowls and arrange the chorizo slices around the edges. Place a poussin breast and two legs on top of each serving. Drizzle around the reserved cooking oil and serve immediately with a herb green salad, if liked.

breast of chicken
on pumpkin and parmesan puree

SERVES 4

1 small pumpkin,
about 2¹/₄ lbs. in total ●

8 tablespoons olive oil

1 onion, finely chopped ●

4 chicken breast supremes ●
(on the bone with skin on)

2 cups (5 oz.) freshly shredded ●
Parmesan

11 oz. chanterelle mushrooms, ●
wiped clean and tough
stalks trimmed

3 tablespoons chopped fresh
flat-leaf parsley ●

Preheat the oven to 350°F. Peel the pumpkin with a vegetable peeler or sharp knife. Cut into quarters and remove the pips; discard, then cut the flesh into small cubes. Heat a large saucepan. Add two tablespoons of the olive oil, then add the onion. Cook for 2–3 minutes until softened but not colored, then tip in the pumpkin cubes.

Cook the pumpkin for another 5 minutes or so until just beginning to soften, stirring occasionally to prevent the mixture sticking to the bottom of the saucepan. Season to taste, then pour in 1³/₄ cups (14 fl.oz.) of water and bring to a boil. Reduce the heat and simmer for another 15–20 minutes or until the pumpkin is completely tender. Drain off any excess water.

Heat an ovenproof skillet until very hot. Season the chicken breasts. Add two tablespoons of olive oil and then add the chicken breasts, skin-side down. Cook for 1–2 minutes until the skin is lightly golden, then turn over and cook for another couple of minutes until lightly seared all over. Place in the oven for 8–10 minutes until the chicken is tender and cooked through. Leave to rest in a warm place for 3–4 minutes.

Meanwhile, blitz the pumpkin mixture with a hand-held blender until smooth, then pass through a sieve into a clean saucepan. If it is too thin, then reduce for another 5–10 minutes until thick, stirring occasionally. Remove from the heat, stir in the Parmesan and season to taste, then cover and keep warm.

Heat a heavy-based skillet. Add two tablespoons of the olive oil and then tip in the chanterelles. Stir-fry for 1 minute, then season and tip in two tablespoons of the parsley. Continue to cook for a few more minutes until tender and all the liquid has been absorbed back into the mushrooms.

Divide the pumpkin puree between warmed wide-rimmed serving bowls and place a piece of chicken on top. Spoon around the chanterelle mushrooms and drizzle a little olive oil to each one. Garnish with the rest of the parsley and serve immediately.

There's nothing nicer than a good chicken pie. Mind you, the first thing you need is some really good chicken, ideally free-range or, better still, organic. I first tasted this served at Kate O'Brien's in San Francisco and had written down the recipe before I even left the table. Obviously you can make your own puff pastry but the frozen shop-bought variety is a good alternative and can save a good deal of time.

jerry burns chicken and leek pot pie

SERVES 4

1 tablespoon olive oil

1 lb. skinless chicken breast fillets, diced ●

1 leek, cut into 1-inch slices ●

2 oz. (about 2) shallots, sliced ●

2 oz. (about 1/2) potato, diced ●

5 tablespoons (3 fl.oz.) heavy cream, plus a little extra for glazing ●

1 lb. puff pastry, thawed if frozen, plus a little all-purpose flour for dusting ●

Preheat the oven to 375°F. Heat a large saucepan. Add the olive oil and sauté the chicken for a couple of minutes until just tender and lightly browned.

Add the leeks to the saucepan with the shallots and potatoes, then season generously and cook gently for 6–8 minutes or until the potatoes are completely tender and cooked through, stirring occasionally to ensure that the potatoes don't stick to the saucepan.

Pour the cream into the saucepan, bring to a simmer and then cook gently for a few minutes until the sauce has reduced and slightly thickened. Pour into a 2-pint pie dish and allow to cool completely. Roll out the puff pastry on a lightly floured board and cut a thin strip off the edge of the pastry, brush with a little water and press it on to the rim of the pie dish to help form a crust.

Stamp out 2³/4-inch circles from the remaining pastry with a straight-sided cutter. Brush the rim with a little more water and use the pastry circles to cover the filling completely, using a little water to help the circles stick together as you go.

Using a sharp knife, make some incisions into the pastry and brush with a little cream to help form a glaze. Place in the oven for 25–30 minutes or until the pastry is puffed up and golden brown. Bring the pie to the table and serve straight from the dish on to warmed serving plates with some buttered peas, if liked.

take 6
ingredients | poultry and game

There are so many different recipes for chili, and so many differing opinions as to the correct version. Well, this is a fairly straightforward recipe but it's pretty damn good. Increase the quantities and it's perfect for feeding a crowd or a wonderful freezer standby for nights when you're craving a spicy TV supper. If you are being very health conscious you could reduce the quantity of olive oil and try to find a low-fat sour cream or use Greek strained yogurt instead.

turkey and black bean chili

SERVES 4

2 tablespoons olive oil

1 lb. lean minced turkey breast ●

1–2 red chiles, pitted and finely ● chopped

2 x 14 oz. cans of black-eyed ● beans, drained and rinsed

2 x 14 oz. cans whole peeled ● plum tomatoes, drained, and flesh diced

4 heaped tablespoons ● sour cream

1½ cups (4 oz.) mature ● Cheddar cheese, shredded

Heat a skillet. Add the oil to the skillet and sauté the minced turkey for 2–3 minutes until just tender, breaking up any lumps with the back of a wooden spoon.

Add the chile or chiles to the skillet, depending on how hot you like your chili and cook for another minute or so, stirring. Stir in the beans and allow to heat through, then add the tomatoes, season and bring to a boil. Reduce the heat and simmer for 5–10 minutes until the sauce has reduced and thickened slightly and the turkey is completely tender.

Season the turkey and black bean chili to taste and spoon into warmed wide-rimmed bowls. Add a spoonful of the sour cream to each serving and scatter the Cheddar cheese on top. Serve at once with tortilla chips, if liked.

take 6
ingredients | poultry and game

A classic Indian restaurant dish, simple, with lovely tastes and textures. I like to serve it with a fresh, crispy cucumber salad, but be warned: everyone will be back for second helpings. Try to buy free-range chicken breasts for this recipe as they are much more juicy and full of flavor.

tandoori chicken kebabs with mango

SERVES 4

4 tablespoons tandoori paste ●

4 tablespoons lime juice ●

²/₃ cup (¹/₄ pint) natural yogurt ●

1¹/₂ lbs. skinless chicken breast ●
fillets, cut into 1¹/₂-inch cubes

1 large, ripe mango, peeled and ●
flesh cut into 1-inch chunks

A little olive oil

4 tablespoons chopped ●
fresh cilantro

Place the tandoori paste in a bowl and add the lime juice and half of the yogurt. Season to taste and beat until well combined. Thread the chicken alternately with the mango on to wooden skewers. Arrange in a shallow non-metallic dish and pour over the yogurt mixture, turning to coat. Cover with plastic wrap and chill for at least 2 hours or overnight is fine.

Heat a griddle pan until hot. Brush with a little olive oil, then add the chicken kebabs and cook for 6–8 minutes or until the chicken is tender and lightly charred. Arrange on warmed serving plates with some cucumber salad, if liked. Drizzle over the remaining yogurt and garnish with the chopped fresh cilantro. Serve at once.

I always keep a packet of flour tortillas in the cupboard – they often come in handy. To make them soft enough for rolling, place them under the broiler or on a skillet or griddle pan. Alternatively, they can also be microwaved on high between dampened sheets of paper towels for about 20 seconds. You can use either chicken breast fillets or my preference: boneless chicken thighs which have a much more succulent flavor and, of course, are cheaper.

chicken tortillas with avocado, chile and sour cream

SERVES 2

14 oz. boneless, skinless chicken, diced

2 tablespoons olive oil

4 soft flour tortillas, each about 8 inches in diameter

2 heaped tablespoons sour cream

2 ripe avocados

1 ripe tomato, peeled, pitted and diced

1 red chile, pitted and finely chopped

Preheat the broiler or a griddle pan. Thread the chicken on to soaked wooden skewers, making sure they are not too tightly packed together. Brush with the olive oil and cook for 4–5 minutes, depending on the size of the dice or until the chicken is completely tender and lightly charred. Leave until cool enough to handle.

Place the tortillas on the broiler rack and then place under the broiler for 30 seconds to 1 minute to just warm through, turning once. Alternatively, use the griddle pan.

Meanwhile, remove the chicken from the skewers. Peel the avocados and then cut each one in half and remove the pips. Cut the flesh into 1/2-inch dice. Spread the softened tortillas with the sour cream and scatter the chicken down the center of each one. Place the avocado on top with the tomato dice and chile, then roll up to enclose the filling completely.

Return to the broiler rack and place under the broiler, seam-side down for 1–2 minutes until the tops are lightly toasted; or use the griddle pan. Cut each tortilla in half on the diagonal and arrange on warmed serving plates. Serve immediately.

take 6 ingredients | poultry and game

Transfer the bell pepper halves to a bowl with tongs and cover with plastic wrap – this will help the skins to steam off. Leave to cool completely, then peel away the skins and discard. Roughly chop the bell pepper flesh, and place in a small saucepan with ½ cup (4 fl.oz.) of the broth. Simmer until reduced by half, then blitz with a hand-held blender until smooth and thickened. Season to taste and set aside.

Preheat the oven to 350°F. Heat an ovenproof skillet until hot. Season the stuffed chicken fillets. Add two tablespoons of the olive oil, and then add the stuffed chicken fillets, skin-side down. Cook for 1–2 minutes until the skin is lightly golden, then turn over and cook for another couple of minutes until lightly seared all over. Place in the oven for 6–8 minutes, until the chicken is just tender and cooked through. Leave to rest in a warm place for 3–4 minutes.

Place the remaining broth in a saucepan and bring to a boil. Place the cous cous in a bowl and pour in the boiling broth, then cover tightly with plastic wrap and set aside for 5 minutes. Remove the plastic wrap, and fork through to remove any lumps. Add enough of the red bell pepper coulis to moisten and color the cous cous. Season to taste. Reheat in a sauté pan, stirring gently to ensure you don't break any of the grains.

Spoon the cous cous into 4-inch cooking rings set in the middle of warmed wide-rimmed bowls. Carefully carve each stuffed chicken breast at an angle and arrange one on top of each pile of cous cous. Drizzle around a few drops of the remaining olive oil and garnish with fresh chervil sprigs, if liked.

Perfect for a picnic on the lawn or an al fresco summer lunch. This dish relies on good
ingredients to make a simple dish great. Although this recipe may look involved it
really is an easy dish to cook with all of the work being done beforehand, allowing
you plenty of time to enjoy with your guests.

corn-fed chicken stuffed with goat
cheese and vine-ripened tomatoes

SERVES 4

4 firm, small vine-ripened
tomatoes ●

6 tablespoons olive oil

1 cup (7 oz.) soft goat cheese ●

4 x medium (4–5 oz.) corn-fed ●
chicken breast fillets, skin on

5 red bell peppers ●

1 1/3 cups (12 fl.oz.) chicken ●
broth (preferably home-made)

1 1/3 cups (8 oz.) cous cous ●

Preheat the oven to 225°F. Cut the tomatoes in half, through the stalk, and then cut out
the green eye from each half. Lay the tomatoes on a baking sheet, cut-side up, and
sprinkle with a little seasoning, then drizzle over a tablespoon of the olive oil. Place the
tomatoes in the oven (you may have to prop the door open slightly to keep the
temperature down). Leave for 2–4 hours until the tomatoes have reduced to about half
their original size but are not at all colored. Turn them over and leave for another 1–2
hours or until they are nice and firm, but again, not at all colored. Remove from the
oven and leave to cool.

Mash the goat cheese to break it down and season to taste. Take each chicken breast
and using a sharp knife make an incision under the small fillet large enough to form a
small pocket. Stuff each pocket with the goat cheese and two pieces of the home-dried
tomatoes. Season and fold over the pocket to cover the filling. Place on a plate, cover
with plastic wrap, and chill for at least 30 minutes or overnight is fine to allow the
filling to firm up.

Preheat the broiler until very hot. Cut the bell peppers in half and remove the pips,
stalk and inner membrane. Sprinkle a roasting pan with sea salt and a tablespoon of the
olive oil. Place the bell peppers cut side down on the tray and drizzle another
tablespoon of oil on top. Place under the broiler and cook for about 10 minutes or until
the skins are blackened and blistered.

take 6
ingredients | poultry and
game

vegetables

Ideally sweetcorn should be cooked the moment it is picked, as the sugar soon converts to starch. The juicy sweetness is lost, so in an ideal world, you should put a large saucepan of water on the stove to bring to a boil, then go out and cut the cobs! But not many of us can do that which is why it is one of the few vegetables that I would recommend using frozen if you don't have access to a good greengrocers who guarantees a swift supply. Serve this dish as an accompaniment to roast meat or game. Smoked chile butter can also be used to flavor risottos, couscous, pastas and soups.

smoked chile-buttered
corn on the cob

SERVES 4

2 teaspoons (1/2 oz.) smoked dried chiles

1/4 cup (1/2 stick) unsalted butter, softened

2 teaspoons (1/2 oz.) chopped fresh red chile (pips removed)

1 teaspoon freshly grated ginger root

2 tablespoons (1 oz.) chopped fresh cilantro

4 large corn on the cob (preferably fresh, frozen will do)

Place the dried chiles in a small saucepan with enough olive oil to just cover. Warm through gently, then leave to soak and reconstitute for at least 15 minutes or up to a couple of hours is fine. Drain the chiles, then finely chop, reserving the olive oil to use for cooking or in dressings.

Place the butter in a bowl with the dried and fresh chiles, the ginger and cilantro. Mix until well combined, then spoon on to a sheet of plastic wrap in the shape of a log or sausage. Roll up the plastic wrap to enclose the butter completely, then twist the ends to secure. Chill for at least 2 hours to firm up or up to 2 days is fine.

When you are ready to serve, cook the corn in a large saucepan of boiling, salted water for 10–15 minutes or until tender, just be careful not to overcook it – when corn is in season it normally takes less time to cook. Drain from the saucepan and place on warmed serving plates. Cut thin slices of the flavored butter and arrange on top. Serve at once, just as the butter is beginning to melt.

take 6
ingredients | vegetables

These make an excellent accompaniment to club sandwiches or just about anything really. Although they do cool down quite quickly, they are also excellent served cold and will sit happily at room temperature for a couple of hours. You really need a mandolin to prepare the potatoes as it is extremely difficult to get them right by hand. However, Chinese mandolins have come down in price in recent years and you should be able to pick one up for a reasonable price.

curried shoestring potatoes

in newspaper

SERVES 4

2 lbs. (about 6) large potatoes ●

2 level tablespoons (1 oz.) ●
curry powder

4 garlic cloves, ●
peeled and sliced

2 tablespoons of aïoli ●
(preferably home-made,
see recipe on page 123)

Heat the vegetable oil to 375°F in an electric deep-fat fryer or large saucepan (use a cooking thermometer if necessary).

While the oil is heating, prepare the potatoes. Peel the potatoes and using the mandolin, cut them into long, thin strips so they resemble shoestrings (fine julienne).

Place the potatoes in a large bowl and sprinkle over the curry powder and add the sliced garlic, tossing to combine. Set aside for 3–5 minutes until the starch begins to leak from the potatoes and the mixture starts to look sticky.

Deep fry the potatoes for 3–4 minutes until golden brown (discarding the sliced garlic). Drain on plenty of paper towels and season to taste. Pile them into newspaper cones that are set on warmed serving plates, drizzle over the aïoli and serve at once.

take 6
ingredients | vegetables

Baby leeks are wonderful vegetables and have now become more widely available. They are one of my favorite vegetables when they first appear in autumn and early winter. Their delicate yet distinctive, mildly oniony flavor makes them the perfect accompaniment to all meat dishes, not to mention poultry or fish. When preparing them, simply trim away any ragged or damaged tops and trim down the stalks.

braised baby leeks with tapenade

SERVES 4

1/2 cup (3 oz.) black olives, stoned (good quality)

2 large garlic cloves, finely chopped

2 teaspoons (1/2 oz.) canned anchovy fillets, finely chopped

2 teaspoons (1/2 oz.) sun-dried tomatoes, chopped (preserved in brine)

About 3 tablespoons olive oil

18 (1 lb.) baby leeks, trimmed

Place the olives in a food processor or liquidizer with the garlic, anchovies, sun-dried tomatoes and three tablespoons of olive oil, then blend to a smooth paste. Season to taste and add a little more oil if you think the tapenade is too thick – it should be the consistency of thick heavy cream.

Place the leeks in a pan of boiling salted water and cook for 2–4 minutes or until lightly cooked and just tender – the exact cooking time will depend on their size. Drain and quickly refresh in a bowl of ice-cold water, then pat dry with paper towels and arrange in a warmed serving dish. Drizzle over the tapenade and serve at once.

take 6
ingredients | vegetables

desserts

This is an incredibly easy dessert, best made in the cold depths of winter when mangoes are cheap and at their best. You can jazz it up by serving it with a selection of exotic fruit. Coconut cream is now readily available in most major supermarkets in 7fl oz tetra packs, but if you have trouble finding it, simply place a can of coconut milk in the freezer for half an hour and allow it to settle, then carefully spoon off the cream, which will have risen to the top.

coconut rice pudding with mango

SERVES 8

2 vanilla pods ●

2 cups (18 fl. oz.) coconut ● cream

²/₃ cup (¹/₄ pint) heavy cream ●

²/₃ cup (5 oz.) superfine sugar, ● plus a little extra, if necessary

²/₃ cup (4 oz.) short grain ● pudding rice

2 ripe mangoes ●

To make the rice pudding, cut the vanilla pods in half and place them in a heavy saucepan. Add the coconut cream, 4 tablespoons (2 fl. oz.) of the heavy cream and ¹/₂ cup (4 oz.) of the sugar and bring slowly to a boil. Stir in the rice, bring back to a boil and simmer very gently for 45 minutes to 1 hour until it has thickened and the rice is tender, stirring occasionally. Remove from the heat, leave to cool, then cover with plastic wrap and chill for at least 2 hours or overnight is fine.

To make the mango coulis, peel the mangoes and then cut away the flesh from the pits and cut into chunks. Place in a food processor or liquidizer with a tablespoon of water and blend to a puree. Transfer to a pan and add the remaining sugar. Bring to a boil, stirring, then simmer for a minute or so until the sugar has dissolved. Taste for sweetness (this will depend on the ripeness of the mango) and add a little more if necessary. Pass the mango puree through a fine sieve into a jug, cover with plastic wrap and chill – you should have about a cup (8 fl. oz.) of coulis in total. If you find that the coulis is too thick, then just add a little water to thin it down.

Whip the remaining cream in a bowl to soft peaks. Remove the vanilla pods from the rice pudding and then fold in the whipped cream to help create a lighter texture.

Pour the mango coulis into wide-rimmed bowls. Quickly dip two tablespoons into boiling water and use to shape the rice pudding into a quenelle (oval ball). Place a quenelle of rice pudding on each pool of coulis to serve.

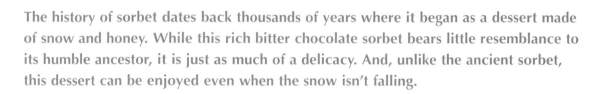

The history of sorbet dates back thousands of years where it began as a dessert made of snow and honey. While this rich bitter chocolate sorbet bears little resemblance to its humble ancestor, it is just as much of a delicacy. And, unlike the ancient sorbet, this dessert can be enjoyed even when the snow isn't falling.

bitter chocolate sorbet

with raspberries

SERVES 4–6

²/₃ cup (5 oz.) superfine sugar ●

2¹/₂ tablespoons (1¹/₂ oz.) ●
liquid glucose

¹/₃ cup (3¹/₂ fl. oz.) milk ●

2 tablespoons (1¹/₄ oz.) cocoa ●
powder (good quality)

4 squares (3¹/₂ oz.) dark ●
chocolate (70 percent cocoa
solids), finely chopped

2 cups (1 lb.) fresh raspberries ●

Place the sugar in a heavy saucepan with 1¹/₂ cups (14 fl. oz.) of water, the liquid glucose, milk and cocoa powder. Bring to a boil, stirring from time to time, then simmer for 2 minutes, whisking constantly to prevent the bottom of the saucepan from catching.

Remove the saucepan from the heat and add the chocolate, stirring until the chocolate has melted. Pass through a fine sieve into a jug, cover with plastic wrap and chill for a few hours until it is really cold.

Now you can either churn the mixture in an ice-cream machine or pour it into a plastic container and freeze until it is almost firm. If doing the latter, scrape the mixture into a food processor and whizz until smooth. Pour it back into the plastic container and repeat one more time. Return the sorbet to the freezer and freeze until firm.

To serve, quickly dip two tablespoons into boiling water and use to shape the sorbet into quenelles (oval balls). Arrange three in each wide rimmed serving bowl and decorate with the raspberries. Serve immediately.

take 6
ingredients | desserts

The sweet blackcurrants with their hint of acidity, complement the goat cheese perfectly in this heavenly soufflé. As with all soufflés, butter the mold well and don't over-whisk the egg whites or you won't get a perfect rise. Serve it immediately – there's no hanging around with this dessert.

blackcurrant soufflé

with goat cheese

SERVES 4

1 cup (8 oz.) blackcurrants ●

²/₃ cup (5 oz.) superfine sugar, ● plus extra for dusting

Knob of unsalted butter ●

3 egg whites ●

1 tablespoon (³/₄ oz.) soft mild ● goat cheese (chèvre)

Confectioners' sugar, to dust ●

Preheat the oven to 400°F. Place the blackcurrants in a food processor or liquidizer and whizz to a puree, then pass through a fine sieve to achieve a smooth puree – you'll need 3¹/₂ oz. in total. Place in a pan with ¹/₄ cup (2 oz.) of the sugar and simmer gently for about 5 minutes until well reduced to a tar-like consistency, stirring occasionally. Leave to cool.

Lightly grease a soufflé dish that is 6 inches in diameter x 2¹/₂ inches high with the butter and then dust with superfine sugar. Place the egg whites in a large bowl and whisk to soft peaks, then gradually whisk in the remaining superfine sugar until thickened and glossy. Fold in the cooled blackcurrant mixture and carefully pour into the prepared soufflé dish.

Press the goat cheese into the middle of the soufflé and smooth over the top with a palette knife. Place on a baking sheet and bake for 15–20 minutes or until well risen and lightly golden, but still soft in the middle. Test by giving the dish a slight shake or push. If it wobbles alarmingly it needs another few minutes; if is fairly steady, then it is ready. Dust lightly with confectioners' sugar and bring straight to the table to serve.

take**6**
ingredients | desserts

This is a variation on one of my all-time favorite desserts and, without a doubt, one of easiest – you can even make it all in advance. The pears improve with keeping, making this an excellent dessert for a dinner party. If you want to serve them warm, just heat them gently in a saucepan, but do not let them boil.

poached pears in red wine
with mint fromage frais

SERVES 4

- 1½ cups (14 fl. oz.) red wine
- 1⅓ cups (11 oz.) superfine sugar
- Juice of 3 oranges
- 4 large firm, ripe pears
- ¾ cup (5 oz.) fromage frais (blanc)
- 2 tablespoons finely chopped fresh mint, plus 4 tiny sprigs to decorate

Heat a heavy saucepan. Pour in the red wine and simmer until reduced by half. Pour in 4 cups (1¾ pints) of water and then add nearly all of the sugar (keeping back 2 tablespoons) and the orange juice. Bring to a boil and simmer for 5 minutes until the sugar has completely dissolved, stirring occasionally.

Reduce the temperature of the pan. Peel the pears using a potato peeler, keeping the stalks intact, then, using a melon baller, scoop out the pips and pith from the bottom of the pears before placing them in the simmering liquid, stalks upwards. Simmer gently for 25–30 minutes or until the pears are tender and the syrup has reduced by half. To test this, simply pierce one of the pears with a small sharp knife – if it goes in easily then it is cooked.

Carefully transfer the pears to a wire rack with a slotted spoon and allow them to cool. Boil the remaining syrup for another 5–10 minutes or until it has reduced to a coating-sauce consistency. Leave to cool, stirring occasionally to prevent a skin forming.

Place the fromage frais in a bowl and sweeten to taste with the remaining 2 tablespoons sugar, then stir in the chopped mint. Cover with plastic wrap and chill until ready to use.

To serve, place a poached pear in the center of each wide-rimmed bowl and spoon over a little of the red wine syrup. Decorate each pear at the stalk with a tiny mint sprig. Quickly dip two tablespoons into boiling water and use to shape the mint fromage frais into quenelles (oval balls). Arrange at the side of the pears to serve.

These chocolate fondants can be made well in advance, as they improve if they have been allowed to rest for at least three hours before baking. If you have the luxury of an extra serving it is always a good idea to use it as a 'tester' after cooking. The mixture should be still soft in the center, but able to hold its own shape. If it begins to collapse at all; simply cook the remaining fondants for a few more minutes.

hot chocolate fondants

SERVES 6

1 cup (2¹/₄ sticks) unsalted butter, plus extra for greasing ●

2 tablespoons (1¹/₄ oz.) cocoa powder, plus extra for dusting ●

9 squares (9 oz.) dark chocolate (70 percent cocoa solids) ●

1 heaped cup (4³/₄ oz.) all-purpose flour ●

2 eggs ●

³/₄ cup (7 oz.) superfine sugar ●

Grease 6 x 7 fl. oz. dariole molds with a little butter and then dust with cocoa powder. Set aside. Break the chocolate into pieces and place in a large heatproof bowl set over a pan of simmering water. Allow to melt and then gradually whisk in the butter. Set aside and allow to cool a little.

Sieve the flour and cocoa powder into a bowl. Whisk the eggs and sugar in another bowl until pale and fluffy, then fold into the cooled chocolate mixture until well combined. Finally fold in the flour mixture and either pipe or spoon into the prepared dariole molds until each one is no more than three-quarters full, gently tapping to remove any air bubbles. Cover with plastic wrap and chill for at least 3 hours or up to 5 hours is fine.

Preheat the oven to 400°F. Arrange the dariole molds on a baking sheet and bake for 12–14 minutes. Leave to rest for a minute or two, then invert each dariole mold into the middle of a wide-rimmed bowl and serve immediately with a spoonful of whipped cream and some warmed chocolate sauce, if liked.

take 6
ingredients | desserts

This chocolate torte is very rich and very moreish. With a creamy bitt...
center and pastry that melts in your mouth, this tart is delicious accom...
dollop of whipped cream. Be warned, there will be requests for secon...

chocolate torte

SERVES 8

1 lb. ready-made sweet shortcrust
pastry, thawed if frozen

Cocoa powder, to dust

2/3 cup (1/4 pint) milk

2 1/2 cups (1 pint) heavy cream

14 squares (14 oz.) dark
chocolate (70 percent cocoa
solids), finely chopped

2 eggs

Preheat the oven to 400°F. Roll out the pastry until it is about 1/8-inch th...
surface lightly dusted with cocoa powder. Cut it into a circular shape, s...
than the diameter of a 10-inch flan ring. Press the pastry into the flan ri...
baking sheet and chill for 15 minutes.

Line the pastry ring with parchment paper and fill with baking beans, th...
10–12 minutes until the pastry is 'set' but not colored. Remove from the...
out the parchment paper and baking beans. Return the pastry case to th...
bake for a further 8–10 minutes until the pastry is lightly golden. Remove...
and leave to cool completely.

Reduce the oven temperature to 275°F. Place the milk and 1 cup (9 fl. o...
in a heavy saucepan and bring to a boil. Add the chocolate, remove fro...
allow the chocolate to melt, stirring occasionally. Leave to cool to room...
Lightly whisk the eggs and then gently whisk into the chocolate mixture...
baked pastry case and bake for about 30 minutes until the tart is slightly...
the edges and just firm in the center.

Place the remaining cream in a bowl and whip to soft peaks. Remove t...
oven and allow it to cool a little before turning it out, then cut into slice...
slice of torte on a serving plate and add a dollop of the whipped cream...
Serve immediately.

take 6
ingredients | desserts

The vanilla cream chantilly is very rich and very moreish. It can be made a couple of days in advance if you wish. The vanilla pods don't have to be discarded and can make excellent vanilla sugar with very little effort. Simply rinse them well and leave to dry completely, then push deep into a bag or jar of granulated sugar and set aside for a couple of weeks before using.

prunes soaked in armagnac
with vanilla cream chantilly

SERVES 4

32 dried prunes (Agen or another good-quality variety)

7 tablespoons (3¼ fl. oz.) Armagnac (preferably 10 year old)

1 vanilla pod

½ cup (3½ fl. oz.) heavy cream

½ cup (2 oz.) confectioners' sugar, sifted, plus extra for dusting

4 tiny fresh mint sprigs, to decorate

Make a split in each prune and hook out the pits with the tip of a knife. Reshape the fruit and place in a non-metallic bowl with the Armagnac. Cover with plastic wrap and chill for at least 48 hours, but up to one week is fine as the longer you leave the prunes, the better the flavor.

Cut the vanilla pod in half with a small sharp knife and scrape out the pips. Place the pips in a bowl with the cream and whip to soft peaks. Fold in enough of the confectioners' sugar to sweeten.

To serve, remove the prunes from the Armagnac with tongs and arrange eight in each wide-rimmed bowl. Quickly dip two tablespoons in boiling water and use to shape the vanilla chantilly cream into quenelles (oval balls). Place on top of the prunes, then decorate with the mint sprigs and add a dust of confectioners' sugar to serve.

Choose berries that are in peak condition, their deep colors will contrast superbly with the neutral shade of the sabayon. I use this sabayon in many of my dessert recipes. It is a classic French sauce and once you get the hang of it, it's a doddle to make. It will keep happily for a couple of hours, covered with plastic wrap in the fridge, but after that it starts to lose some of its volume.

mixed berries

with champagne sabayon

SERVES 4

1¼ cups (½ pint) Champagne ●

¼ cup (2 oz.) superfine sugar ●

4 egg yolks ●

½ cup (3½ oz.) blackberries ●

½ cup (3½ oz.) raspberries ●

½ cup (3½ oz.) redcurrants, ●
stalks removed

Place the Champagne in a saucepan with the sugar and simmer for a few minutes until the sugar dissolves, stirring occasionally. Remove from the heat and allow to cool a little.

Place the egg yolks in a large heatproof bowl set over a saucepan of simmering water and whisk until well combined and just heated through. Gradually pour in the Champagne mixture, a little at a time until completely combined, whisking continuously.

Continue to whisk the sabayon until the mixture has doubled in size, being careful not to allow the mixture to become too hot or the sabayon may split – this should take no more than 6–8 minutes. Remove the bowl from the heat and allow to cool.

To serve, preheat the broiler until it is very hot. Arrange the berries in a wide-rimmed dish and spoon over enough of the sabayon to just cover. Place under the broiler for a few minutes until golden. Serve immediately.

take 6
ingredients | desserts

A lovely dessert or perfect for afternoon tea. It's a big slice of light, flaky pastry layered with raspberries and a delicious raspberry cream – need I say more? All right – don't eat too much in one sitting.

mille feuilles with raspberries and raspberry cream

SERVES 4

● 3 gelatine leaves

● 2 cups (1 lb.) fresh raspberries

● ½ cup (2 oz.) confectioners' sugar, sifted, plus extra for dusting

● 13 oz. ready-made puff pastry, thawed if frozen

● 1½ cups (14 fl. oz.) heavy cream

Place the gelatine leaves in a shallow dish and cover with cold water. Set aside to soak for 10 minutes. Place half the raspberries in a food processor or liquidizer and whizz to a puree. Scrape into a pan using a spatula and add the confectioners' sugar. Bring to a simmer, stirring until the sugar has dissolved. Remove from the heat.

Take the gelatine leaves out of the water and squeeze out any excess water. Stir into the raspberry mixture until dissolved, then pass through a fine sieve into a non-metallic bowl. Cover with plastic wrap and chill for at least 2 hours or overnight is best.

Preheat the oven to 450°F. Roll out the pastry on a lightly floured surface to a ⅛-inch thickness. Using a 3in plain cutter, stamp out twelve rounds. Using the back of a table knife, make horizontal cuts into the edges of each round to encourage the layers to form. Place on a dampened baking sheet. Prick the rounds with a fork and chill for 15 minutes.

Bake the pastry rounds for 8–10 minutes or until well risen and lightly golden. Remove from the oven and dust each pastry round with confectioners' sugar, then return to the oven for another minute or two until glazed and golden brown. Transfer to a wire rack to cool.

Meanwhile, place the set raspberry jelly in a food processor or liquidizer and briefly whizz back to a puree. Whip the cream in a large bowl to soft peaks and fold in the raspberry puree to create a mousse-like consistency.

To assemble the mille feuilles, layer up the pastry rounds in threes on serving plates, filled with the raspberry cream, finishing with a pastry layer. Place the remaining raspberries on the outside of the pastry round and serve immediately.

take 6
ingredients | desserts

I love to make this with the wild strawberries that grow widely in the early summer. Though they are quite labor intensive to pick, the intense flavor of the dark ripe fruit is always well worth it, but normally comes at a price. The biscuits can be made 24 hours in advance and kept in an airtight container.

sable biscuits

with strawberries and cream

SERVES 8

2 cups (9 oz.) all-purpose flour ●

1 cup (4¹/₂ oz.) confectioners' sugar, plus extra for dusting ●

¹/₂ cup (³/₄ stick) unsalted ● butter, diced

1 small egg yolk ●

1 cup (8 fl. oz.) heavy cream ●

²/₃ cup (8 oz.) strawberries ●

Sieve the flour and ³/₄ cup (3¹/₂ oz.) of the confectioners' sugar into a large bowl and then rub in the butter until the mixture resembles fine breadcrumbs. Make a well in the center and add the egg yolk, mixing to bind. Turn out on to a lightly floured surface and knead lightly until the mixture comes together in a ball. Wrap in plastic wrap and chill for 1 hour.

Preheat the oven to 225°F. Roll out the sable dough on a lightly floured surface to a ¹/₈-inch thickness. Using a 4-inch cooking ring, stamp out 8 rounds – you'll probably have some sable dough left to use for another day. It keeps well in the fridge for up to two weeks. Place the sable rounds on non-stick baking sheets and chill for 15 minutes, then bake for 15 minutes or until cooked through and golden brown. Leave to cool for a minute or so, then transfer to a wire rack and allow to cool completely.

Place the cream in a bowl and sieve in the remaining confectioners' sugar. Whisk until soft peaks form, then cover with plastic wrap and chill until ready to serve. Choose four small strawberries for decorating and cut in half. Set aside. Slice off the stalk tops and then cut each one in half lengthways.

To assemble, place a sable biscuit on each serving plate and place the cooking ring on top. Line with the strawberry halves, cut side against the ring. Spoon in the chilled sweetened cream and gently press to the edges, keeping the strawberries against the sides. Top with another sable biscuit and decorate with the reserved strawberry halves. Add a light dusting of icing sugar to each one, remove the ring and serve.

strawberry tiramisu

1½ cups (11 oz.) mascarpone cheese

1 cup (9 fl. oz.) heavy cream

1 cup (9 fl. oz.) sweet dessert wine (Sauternes or similar)

6 oz. (about 12) boudoir sponge fingers

1 cup (11 oz.) strawberries, hulled

● Mix together the mascarpone and the cream. Spoon half of the mixture on to the bottom of a serving bowl. Pour the wine into a shallow dish and dip in the sponge fingers before arranging them over the mixture, breaking them up as necessary.

● Cover with half the strawberries and then spread the rest of the mascarpone and cream on the top, smoothing down the top with a palette knife that has been briefly dipped in boiling water. Chill for at least two hours or overnight is fine.

● To serve, scatter over the remaining strawberries and bring to the table for maximum effect. Spoon into glass dishes to serve.

orange granita

SERVES 4

Juice of 6 oranges

⅓ cup (3½ fl. oz.) sweet dessert wine

¼ cup (2 oz.) superfine sugar

1 tablespoon finely chopped fresh ginger root

1 teaspoon earl grey tea leaves

● Place the orange juice in a pan with the wine, sugar and ginger and bring to a boil, stirring until the sugar has dissolved. Stir in the tea leaves, remove from the heat and set aside to infuse for 4 minutes. Strain through a sieve into a shallow rigid plastic container and allow to cool completely.

● Freeze for 1 hour, then remove the container from the freezer and stir the mixture to break up the ice crystals. Return to the freezer and repeat the process until you have a mixture of fine-grained frozen crystals and no liquid. Ideally it should be eaten the minute it has frozen, so make sure that you start the recipe only a couple of hours before you wish to serve it.

● To serve, scrape off layers of the granite with a tablespoon rather than using an ice-cream scoop and spoon into martini glasses set on serving plate.

take **6**
ingredients | desserts

If you can get this recipe right there's no doubt that it is the perfect pudding. You should aim for a soft, fragrant passion fruit filling with a crumbly, crunchy pastry bottom. For the 'best' passion fruit flavor prepare the filling two days in advance and leave it in the fridge. It really gives a more distinctive, pronounced result.

passion fruit tart

SERVES 8

- 12 large passion fruit
- 9 eggs
- 1¹/₃ cups (11 oz.) superfine sugar
- 1 cup (9 fl. oz.) heavy cream
- 1 lb. ready-made sweet shortcrust pastry, thawed if frozen
- Confectioners' sugar, to dust

Cut the passion fruit in half and scoop out all of the pips and juice into a bowl. Strain through a sieve into a jug – you'll need 1 cup (9 fl. oz.) of strained juice in total. Break the eggs into a large bowl and lightly whisk to combine, then whisk in the sugar and stir in the passion fruit juice. Whip the cream in a separate bowl to soft peaks and then carefully fold into the passion fruit mixture. Cover with plastic wrap and chill for at least 2 hours or up to two days is fine.

Preheat the oven to 400°F. Roll out the pastry until it is about ¹/₈-inch thick on a work surface lightly dusted with icing sugar. Cut it into a circular shape, slightly larger than the diameter of a 10-inch flan ring. Press the pastry into the flan ring, and place it on a baking sheet and chill for 15 minutes.

Line the pastry ring with parchment paper, fill with baking beans and bake for 10–12 minutes until the pastry is set, but not colored. Remove from the oven and take out the parchment paper and baking beans. Return the pastry case to the oven and bake for a further 8–10 minutes until the pastry is lightly golden. Remove from the oven and leave to cool completely.

Reduce the oven temperature to 225°F. Pour the chilled passion fruit mixture into the baked pastry case and bake for 15–20 minutes until just set, but still slightly wobbly in the center. Leave to rest for 2 minutes, then cut into slices and arrange on serving plates. Add a light dusting of icing sugar and serve immediately.

take 6
ingredients | desserts

This is a really tasty marriage of pears and buttery caramel. It's best served warm with a scoop of vanilla ice cream, but a dollop of whipped cream or sour cream also works well. I like to use a heavy ovenproof skillet for this recipe, but a classic tart tatin mold or shallow cake pan (not a loose-based one) that is about 1/8in thick would be fine; no thicker than 1/4in would also work as well.

pear tarte tatin

SERVES 6–8

Confectioners' sugar, for dusting

8 oz. ready-made puff pastry, thawed if frozen

2¹/₄ lb. (about 5–7) firm, ripe pears

¹/₂ cup (4 oz.) vanilla sugar (see page 141 for home-made recipe)

¹/₄ cup (¹/₂ stick) unsalted butter, at room temperature

6–8 scoops vanilla ice cream, to serve (good quality)

Lightly dust the work surface with confectioners' sugar and then roll out the pastry to a ¹/₈-inch thickness and to a circular shape, 1 inch larger than a 9–10-inch ovenproof skillet. Place on a baking sheet and chill for 30 minutes.

Preheat the oven to 325°F. Peel, core and halve the pears. Heat the vanilla sugar in the ovenproof skillet. When the sugar is golden add the butter, swirling to combine, then add the pear halves and sauté for about 5 minutes until well coated in the caramel. Leave to cool a little, then arrange the pears, cut-side up tightly in the skillet. Leave to cool completely.

Lay the chilled pastry sheet over the top of the pears, tucking in the edges and turning them down so that when the tart is turned out, the edges will create a rim that will hold in the caramel and pear juices. Bake for 25–30 minutes until the pastry is golden brown and the pears are completely tender, but still holding their shape.

Leave the tart in the skillet for a minute or two, then loosen the edges with a round-bladed knife and invert on to a flat serving plate. Rearrange any loose pears back into place with a palette knife and leave to cool, if time allows. This enables all the juices to be reabsorbed and allows the caramel to set slightly because of the pectin in the pears.

To serve, cut the tart into slices and serve on warmed serving plates with a scoop of the vanilla ice cream. This tart can also be re-heated in the oven for 5–10 minutes if you'd prefer to serve it warm.

These golden caramels make a perfect ending to any special meal. The gold leaf topping obviously has the wow factor. They keep perfectly well for up to 3 weeks in a cool place, but they will need to be individually wrapped or arranged on double sheets of greaseproof paper, well spaced apart to prevent them from sticking, in an airtight container. But I normally find they don't last long enough – they are very addictive and should be kept out of the way of children and adults alike!

golden caramels

MAKES ABOUT 2¼ LBS.

½ stick (2 oz.) unsalted butter, plus a little extra for greasing ●

1 vanilla pod ●

2½ cups (1 pint) heavy cream ●

¾ cup (8fl oz) light corn syrup ●

2 cups (14 oz.) granulated sugar ●

½ teaspoon salt

24-carat gold leaf sheet ●

Lightly butter a 9-inch square baking pan and line the base and sides with waxed paper. Using a sharp knife, cut the vanilla pod in half and then scrape out the pips using a small teaspoon. Place in a large heavy saucepan with the cream. Bring to a simmer, stirring continuously, then remove from the heat and set aside to allow the flavors to infuse.

Place the corn syrup in a separate saucepan with the sugar and heat gently, stirring occasionally until the sugar has dissolved. Bring to a boil, without stirring and simmer for about 10 minutes until it has heated to 305°F – check with a sugar thermometer.

When the correct temperature is reached, add the butter and salt to the pan, then stirring constantly slowly pour in the infused cream, making sure that the mixture does not stop boiling. Once all the cream has been added the mixture should become foamy and create a lot of steam.

Reduce the heat of the saucepan until the sugar thermometer registers at 250°F, then cook gently for another 15 minutes or so, stirring occasionally to prevent the mixture from sticking to the bottom of the saucepan. Remove the caramel from the heat and leave to cool for 5 minutes, then pour into the prepared baking pan and leave to set at room temperature for at least 5 hours.

After the caramel has been allowed to set, turn out on to a clean chopping board and using a sharp knife, cut into 1–1½-inch strips, then cut across to form squares. To apply the gold leaf, use a small artist's brush and carefully apply by lifting tiny bits of the gold leaf and brushing it on top of each caramel. Arrange on a serving plate and serve with coffee after a meal.

This lime bavarois uses a little gelatine to help it keep its shape and consistency. However, go easy on the gelatine; it is only there to hold the lightness between making the dessert and eating it. Use too much and the dessert will have an unpleasant, rubbery texture. Thin-skinned limes yield the most juice, as do slightly older ones, recognized by their muddy yellow color. You'll need about four for this recipe in total.

lime bavarois

SERVES 4

2¹/₂ gelatine leaves ●

1 cup (3¹/₂ oz.) confectioners' ● sugar, sifted

³/₄ cup (7 fl. oz.) freshly ● squeezed lime juice

1 cup (9 fl. oz.) heavy cream ●

Place the gelatine leaves in a shallow dish and pour over enough cold water to cover. Set aside to soak for 10 minutes.

Put the sugar in a heavy saucepan with the lime juice. Bring to a simmer, stirring until the sugar has dissolved. Take the soaked gelatine leaves out of the water and squeeze out any excess water, then add to the pan and whisk until dissolved.

Remove the lime mixture from the heat, pour into a non-metallic bowl and leave to cool completely, then cover with plastic wrap and chill for at least 2 hours or overnight.

When the lime mixture has set, whip the cream in a bowl until you have achieved soft peaks. Tip the lime mixture into a food processor or liquidizer and whizz briefly until smooth, then pour into a bowl.

Quickly fold the cream into the blitzed lime mixture and then pour into a glass serving bowl. Chill for at least another 2 hours or overnight is best. Serve the bavarois straight from the serving bowl with separate bowls of lightly whipped cream and raspberries.

This can be made up to three or four days in advance and is easy to serve as dessert at the end of a meal. It is a variation on a classic crème caramel and its texture actually reminds me of a kulfi, which is an Indian ice cream made from cream or milk. Dip briefly in a pan of boiling water to help turn out.

pumpkin and pecan crème

SERVES 4

1 lb. slice of fresh pumpkin ●

1/4 cup (1/2 stick) unsalted butter ●

3/4 cup (5 oz.) pecan nuts, ●
plus extra for decoration

6 egg yolks ●

1/3 cup (3 oz.) superfine sugar ●

2 cups (18 fl. oz.) heavy cream ●

Preheat the oven to 375°F. Scoop out the pumpkin pips using a large spoon, then cut the slice of pumpkin in half again crossways. Smear half of the butter all over the flesh and arrange on a baking sheet. Roast for about 1 hour or until completely tender when pierced with a skewer. Remove from the oven and leave to cool, then scoop out the flesh, discarding the skin, and pass it through a fine sieve or vegetable mouli – this amount will give you 5 oz. – the amount you will need for the recipe.

Reduce the oven temperature to 300°F. Place the pecan nuts on a baking sheet and toast in the oven for about 5 minutes, then remove and allow to cool. Place the egg yolks and sugar in a large bowl and whisk until light and fluffy. Place the cream in a saucepan and bring to a boil, then slowly whisk into the egg mixture. Finally fold in the pumpkin puree until smooth and well combined.

Lightly grease 4 x 7 fl. oz. ramekins with the remaining butter, then pour in the pumpkin mixture and decorate with the pecan halves. Place in a bain marie (roasting tin half filled with boiling water) and cover with aluminium foil. Bake for 40–45 minutes until each ramekin is slightly raised around the edges and just set.

Remove the bain marie from the oven and leave to cool completely, then cover each ramekin with plastic wrap and chill for at least 2 hours or overnight is fine. To serve, briefly dip each ramekin into boiling water and turn out on to a serving plate. Decorate with any left-over pecan nuts and serve immediately.

take 6
ingredients | desserts

This lovely translucent jelly looks stunning with the orange segments running through it like jewels. The refreshing kiwi sauce complements the flavor of the oranges perfectly. It really is so very easy to make and I find it a refreshing and stylish way to end a meal.

orange terrine with kiwi sauce

SERVES 6–8

- *8 gelatine leaves* ●
- *6 ripe kiwi fruit* ●
- *³/₄ cup (6 oz.) superfine sugar* ●
- *12 oranges* ●
- *Fresh mint sprigs, to decorate* ●

Place the gelatine leaves in a shallow dish and pour over enough cold water to cover. Set aside to soak for 10 minutes.

Peel and quarter the kiwi fruit and place in a food processor or liquidizer with 2 tablespoons (1 oz.) of the sugar. Blend until smooth, then tip into a bowl and cover with plastic wrap. Chill until ready to use.

Holding one of the oranges over a large bowl to catch the juices, peel and segment, discarding all the white pith, using a sharp serrated knife. Prepare nine of the remaining oranges in the same way, placing the segments in a separate bowl. Squeeze the juice from the two remaining oranges and place in a saucepan with the orange juice that has been caught in the bowl.

Add the remaining sugar to the saucepan with the orange juice, stirring until the sugar has dissolved. Take the soaked gelatine leaves out of the water and squeeze out any excess water, then add to the saucepan and whisk until dissolved. Strain through a sieve lined with clean cheesecloth into a clean bowl to remove any impurities.

Take a wet 1¹/₂-pint non-stick terrine and pour in a layer of the gelatine mixture. Leave to set in the fridge for 10–15 minutes and then arrange a layer of the orange segments on top. Repeat these layers until the ingredients have been used up, gently heating the remaining gelatine mixture in the microwave for a couple of seconds if it begins to firm up. Leave the terrine to set in the fridge overnight or up to 2 days is fine.

To serve the terrine, briefly dip in a basin of boiling water and turn out on to a flat plate. Cut into slices, using a sharp knife that has been briefly dipped in boiling water. Arrange on serving plates and spoon around some of the kiwi puree. Decorate each serving with a mint sprig and serve at once.

take **6**
ingredients | desserts

Pineapple and chocolate are an excellent combination and this mousse tastes great, although a little goes a long way. Any leftovers can be eaten as a soft torte at room temperature. A scoop of good-quality ice cream or a pineapple sorbet will help it slip down a treat. Be careful not to overcook the mousse, test with a fine metal skewer – it should come out clean.

warm pineapple

and chocolate mousse

SERVES 8–10

- 1 pineapple, peeled, cored and cut into 6 even slices (ends discarded)

- 6 squares (6 oz.) dark chocolate (70 percent cocoa solids)

- 7 tablespoons (3^1/$_2$ oz.) unsalted butter, plus extra for greasing

- 4 large eggs

- ^{1}/$_2$ cup (4^1/$_2$ oz.) superfine sugar

- 2 tablespoons (1 oz.) all-purpose flour

Preheat the oven to 400°F. Butter a 9-inch soufflé dish and arrange three of the pineapple slices in the bottom. Break up the chocolate into squares and place in a heatproof bowl set over a pan of simmering water with the butter. Leave to melt, stirring occasionally, then remove from the heat and leave to cool completely.

Separate the eggs and place the yolks in a bowl with the sugar and beat until light and fluffy, then beat in the flour. Fold in the cooled chocolate mixture until just combined.

Place the egg whites in a separate large bowl and whisk until stiff peaks have formed. Fold into the chocolate mixture and then pour half into the pineapple-lined soufflé dish. Carefully arrange the remaining pineapple slices on top and then pour the rest of the chocolate mixture on top to cover completely. Bake for 30 minutes until just set but still has a slight wobble in the middle. Bring straight to the table and spoon into warmed wide-rimmed bowls. Serve at once with scoops of the vanilla ice cream, if liked.

This delicately flavored ice cream should really be churned and eaten on the same day if you want to achieve that smooth, velvety restaurant finish. Otherwise the secret of making good ice cream is to always use a wooden spoon to stir the custard once it is back in the saucepan and use a side-to-side motion rather than a circular one. This moves the custard about more and prevents the scorching and scrambled egg 'thing' that tends to happen in the bottom of the saucepan.

basil sherbet with fresh fruit salad

SERVES 4

2 cups (18 fl. oz.) milk ●

finely grated zest of ½ lime ●

leaves from 1 large, growing ●
basil plant, (about 2 oz. in total)

3½ oz. egg yolks ●

¾ cup (6 oz.) superfine sugar ●

Good selection of prepared ●
seasonal fruits, cut into
bite-sized pieces (such as
paw paw, mango, orange,
strawberries and lime segments)

Place the milk in a heavy saucepan with the lime zest and half of the basil leaves. Bring to a boil, then remove from the heat and set aside to allow the flavors to infuse for 15–20 minutes.

Once the milk mixture has infused, pass it through a fine sieve lined with cheesecloth into a clean saucepan and re-heat gently. Place the egg yolks in a bowl with the sugar and whisk until combined. Slowly pour the heated infused milk over the egg yolk mixture, whisking constantly.

Pour the custard back into a clean saucepan and stir over a low heat for 2–3 minutes until thickened and the custard is coating the back of a spoon. Remove from the heat and set in a bowl filled with iced water until it has cooled down completely – this helps prevent any further cooking of the custard.

Place the cooled custard in a food processor or liquidizer with the remaining basil leaves and blend until the custard is flecked with green. Pass through a sieve lined with a piece of clean cheesecloth into a clean bowl and then transfer to an ice cream machine. Churn according to manufacturer's instructions. Place in the freezer until half an hour before you are ready to serve, then transfer to the fridge to allow it to soften slightly. Arrange scoops in wide-rimmed bowls with a selection of the fruits. This could also be decorated with tuille biscuits, if liked, before serving.

take 6
ingredients | desserts

My variation on a lovely dessert which I can clearly remember from my childhood. We always had it on special occasions and I loved to help with its preparation. Normally I'd put a couple of pears and a good handful of fresh cherries into it, but unfortunately there's no room. However, you can experiment with your own selection of fruit and there's no doubt, that once you've tasted it, you'll understand why it has stood the test of time.

traditional fruit trifle

SERVES 4–6

1 ripe baby pineapple ●

4 dessert apples ●

1/2 cup (4 oz.) superfine sugar ●

7 oz. trifle sponges ●

3 1/2 tablespoons (2 oz.) black cherry jam ●

1 cup (8 oz.) raspberries ●

To prepare the pineapple, cut off the leaf crown and bottom so that it sits flat. Using a sharp knife, remove the skin by cutting down the length of the fruit, then cut the flesh into wedges lengthways, remove the core and cut into dice. Place in a bowl. Peel, core and dice the apples and add to the bowl.

Place the sugar in a large heavy saucepan with 1/2 cup (4 fl. oz.) of water. Bring to a boil, stirring until the sugar has dissolved. Add the pineapple and apple dice and poach for 1 minute and 30 seconds, then immediately remove from the heat. Strain the poached fruit through a sieve set over a bowl to reserve the stock syrup.

Cut the trifle sponges in half and spread with the black cherry jam. Sandwich back together again and then dice into even-sized squares. Place the raspberries in a food processor or liquidizer and blend to a puree, then pass through a sieve set over a bowl to remove the pips.

To layer up the trifle, spoon a little of the raspberry puree into the bottom of tall glasses. Add some of the sponge and top with a couple of tablespoons of the poached fruit. Continue layering in this way until all the ingredients are used up, finishing with a layer of the raspberry puree. Chill for at least 2 hours, or overnight is fine, to set. Place each glass on a serving plate and top with a layer of lightly whipped cream, if liked, to serve.

index